ALSO FROM
FRIENDLY CITY BOOKS

CHILDREN'S

Stretch Like Scarlet
Emily Liner

POETRY

How to Read
Thomas Richardson

SAVOR

Poems for the Tongue

SAVOR

Poems for the Tongue

Brennan Breeland   Stan Galloway

Editors

Friendly City Books
Columbus, Mississippi

Production of this book was made possible through support from the Friendly City Books Community Connection, a special project of the CREATE Foundation.

Copyright © 2024 by Friendly City Books, Inc.

All rights reserved. No part of this publication may be reproduced, distributed, or transmitted in any form or by any means, including photocopying, recording, or other electronic or mechanical methods, without the prior written permission of the publisher, except in the case of brief quotations embodied in critical reviews and certain other noncommercial uses permitted by copyright law.

The poems included in this anthology remain the intellectual property of their respective authors. Each contributor has asserted their moral rights and retains copyright to their work. Some poems in this anthology appear courtesy of the authors and their original publishers, having been previously published in various magazines, journals, and books. The inclusion of previously published material has been duly noted below each poem with citations to the original sources of publication. For permission requests, write to the publisher at the address below.

Friendly City Books
118 5th Street North
Columbus, MS 39701
publishing@friendlycitybooks.com
https://www.friendlycitybooks.com

For information about special discounts for bulk purchases, please contact Friendly City Books at 1-662-570-4247 or publishing@friendlycitybooks.com.

This book is a work of fiction. Names, characters, places, and incidents either are the product of the author's imagination or are used fictitiously. Any resemblance to actual persons, living or dead, events, or locales is entirely coincidental.

ISBN: 979-8-9904330-0-7
First Edition

Cover art "Abundance" by Hannah McCormick
Interior design by Rich Sobolewski
Printed in the United States of America

Library of Congress Cataloging-in-Publication Data
Names: Breeland, Brennan, editor. | Galloway, Stan, editor.
Title: SAVOR: Poetry for the Tongue / edited by Brennan Breeland and Stan Galloway.
Description: First Edition. | Columbus, MS: Friendly City Books, 2024.
Identifiers: ISBN 979-8-9904330-0-7 pbk.
Subjects: LCSH Poetry. | Food in literature. | Anthologies.
Classification: LCCN 2024907122 | DDC 820/.81—dc23

1 2 3 4 5 6 7 8 9

To Mimi, Fa, Mom, Dad, and Nikki—whose cooking has nourished my soul at least as much as it has nourished my body.

- Brennan

To all the words and foods that have nourished me over the years, and those that have prepared them.

- Stan

Contents

Foreword — 1
Brennan Breeland

Diner — 3
Sandra Anfang

Meguro Station Sushi — 4
Bartholomew Barker

Still Life with Apples, Apple Fritters, Calvados — 5
Daisy Bassen

Making Gumbo — 6
Charlie Becker

Bowl of Tangerines — 9
Claire Booker

As The Day Morphs into Dusk — 10
Despy Boutris

Come Eat with Me and Be My Love — 11
Cathy Bryant

Food Porn II: Sweet Potato — 13
Bett Butler

How to Feed the Grieving — 14
Kirsten Casey

How to Savor an Avocado — 16
Gabriel Cleveland

Bone — 17
Terence Culleton

Cooking — 18
Steve Cushman

Desire — 19
John Davis

Pepper Marriage — 20
John Dorroh

Father's Grapefruit — 21
Jennifer Edwards

Dinner with My Ex at the Lucky Noodle — 22
Linda McCauley Freeman

Manners at the Table: How to Eat a Lobster —Boiled or Broiled — 24
Katherine Gaffney

Living Off the Land Around the Bay — 26
Reuven Goldfarb

Dinner at Manresa — 27
Erica Goss

An Ode to Figs in August — 28
Connie Jordan Green

Bourdain Said — 29
George Guida

Kitchen Konkani — 30
Mrinalini Harchandrai

In the Checkout Line at Trader Joe's — 32
J. David Harper

The Liberation of Sunlight and Hope — 33
Mureall Hebert

Seasonal Diet — 35
Emily Hockaday

Macedonian Bean Soup — 36
Karen Paul Holmes

Ghirardelli: San Francisco   37
John Hoppenthaler

Perugian Pear   38
Mary Louise Kiernan

Ode to the Fish-Fry   39
Emilee Kinney

Cultivation   41
Phyllis Klein

Pieces of Silver   42
J.I. Kleinberg

Only a Lady Poet   43
Miriam Kotzin

Carrots   44
Mark L. Levinson

Uvulae   45
Raymond Luczak

Moussaka   46
Linda Malnack

I Love You More Than Popcorn   47
John C. Mannone

BLAT   49
Karen Greenbaum-Maya

On First Eating Crawfish   50
Michael Mingo

Compulsorily Wholesome   51
Thomas Mixon

In Defense of the Apricot   52
Wilda Morris

Don't Bring the Turkey to the Table 53
Jill Munro

Friday Afternoon at Mahane Yehuda Marketplace 54
Sharon Lask Munson

Closed Mouths Don't Get Fed 56
Russell Nichols

Blackberries 57
Arlene Plevin

Ramps 58
Kyle Potvin

How to Braid Challah 59
Claudia M. Reder

Nana Loves to Eat Strawberries 61
Lisa Reynolds

And All God's People Said "Amen" 62
Thomas Richardson

Pistachios 63
Karen Rigby

Pantoum with Catheter and Total Parenteral Nutrition 64
Kim Roberts

Whiskey 65
Wilderness Sarchild

Lemon: An Essence 67
Ellen Sazzman

Chicken of the Woods 68
Carla Schwartz

Singing the Willamette Valley 69
Mistee St. Clair

Cuamochtlis — 71
Mr. Tezozomoc

Returns — 73
Ross Thompson

Leaving Home — 74
Lisa Timpf

Late Night Supper — 75
Kerry Trautman

Truly, Really — 76
Anastasia Vassos

In Praise of Garlic — 77
Elinor Ann Walker

Yeast — 78
Laura Grace Weldon

Some Notes and Three Word Problems on Red Velvet Cake — 79
Kory Wells

Personal Etymology of Mush — 82
Marceline White

Soup Town Days — 83
Jinn Bug & Ron Whitehead

Midwest Corn Roast — 86
Scott Wiggerman

My Brother's Gift of the Palobar Cookbook — 88
Amelia L. Williams

Chanterelles — 90
Susan Wolbarst

Hunger — 91
Christopher Woods

Creation Myth: Toast · 92
Robert Wynne

I Serve it Forth · 93
Sarah Yasin

Grandmother's Kitchen · 94
Hiromi Yoshida

Afterword · 96
Stan Galloway

About the Editors · 97

Contributor Biographies · 98

About Friendly City Books · 113

Foreword

It is often said that we eat first with our eyes.

This is why Instagram feeds overflow with beautifully plated works of culinary art, almost too beautiful to eat. However, it seems to me that we eat first not with our eyes, but with our memories. The beauty of food on a plate is window-dressing applied to an emotional connection, established between those who cook, those who eat, and those who cooked and ate before.

When we first experience the love of family, and as we develop an understanding of that love in our formative years, it is often in the context of food. My grandmother told us she loved us by asking us if we were hungry. She showed us by filling our bellies with the work of her hands.

And when we grew up, life moved past us at an increasingly dizzying pace. In the years since she passed away, we remember her not through pictures or stories, but the scents and flavors we chase as we painstakingly follow her handwritten recipes and the scratched-through cookbooks recipes, incorrect as published but thankfully fixed after the fact in the looping, feverish, distinctive-though-sometimes-illegible cursive of her hand. Cousins check in with aunts and uncles to cross-reference the unreadable, sharing stories, laughing, and crying as we strive—if only for a moment—to transport ourselves back to her kitchen and the feelings of safety and comfort it provided.

So, although food and poetry might not seem like the most intuitive pairing, it has always made sense to me: we express our emotions through the written word, but often, we are more capable of doing so through food. That, in my experience, has been the primary medium of expressing love. And as I developed an interest in poetry, food seemed the obvious lens through which to analyze the human experience in all its breadth, complexity, simplicity, and poignancy.

In light of this, Savor is dedicated to those who feed us, body and soul, with the work of their hands. Grandmas, Nonnas, Aunties, and Sunday-morning-pancake-Dads, sure, but also the nameless, faceless, unsung heroes of the diners, fast-casual spots, and neighborhood restaurants.

Thank you, from those whom you feed so lovingly.

Brennan Breeland
Plainfield, New Jersey

Diner

Every morning I look for you on the menu. Under *Appetizers*, I find no fifty-something man tenderized with love, no well-stitched heart with scars like pennants, no arms to cradle me, honest mouth to speak its truth, laughing eyes to draw me in. I dart into the kitchen where I catch a glimpse as you hightail it out the service entrance. As usual, I'm too late; you're gone for good. Things get worse in *Entrees*. I flip to *Desserts*, consider rhubarb pie for half a second but I know it would only be a cheap thrill. I need sustenance. I settle on two poached eggs slathered in red curry, a dollop of honey goat cheese on the side, and fresh Olallieberries. A slice of sprouted wheat bread with fresh butter and strong Genmaicha tea—make that a double—to finish it off. It's gonna be one of those days.

BARTHOLOMEW BARKER

Meguro Station Sushi

Tuna draped over rice,
a languid beauty
in a red pencil skirt
on a velvet couch
with wasabi trim.

It wasn't a tuna fish
riding the conveyor belt
waiting to be chosen
by a salaryman at lunch.
It was just a slice,
a twitching muscle
filled with hot blood
just a few hours earlier
in the quiet beneath the waves
instead of this harsh afterlife
above the rumble
of the Tokyo Metro.

To honor her unwilling sacrifice
I shall breathe life
back into this flesh,
accept it as my own,
dipped in the dark
of soy sauce.

DAISY BASSEN

Still Life with Apples, Apple Fritters, Calvados
an imaginary ekphrasis

Forget Eden—that was a pomegranate,
Or a fig, maybe an etrog citron, primarily pith.

Forget the teachers you wanted to impress
Or distract from their memories of chalk,

Doctors who could be kept away, oranges
Missing their comrades roundly;

It reminds you of a Vermeer, a golden scale
Tipped by the fruit's heft within your brain,

The scale as real as the apples, apples
Rendered in red ochre, nacarat carmine, vermilion;

It reminds you of the transfiguration of sugar,
Decay, a weak sort of oblivion like a lucid dream;

Dali would screw clock-hands to the ruddy peel
To underscore how regret begins and passes,

Such a busy painting, industrious, invisible
As the work of women, the batter fried in oil,

The brandy made in an alembic. You were wrong
At first glance, in your assumptions.

Forget cleverness, forget philosophy—
Apples, cleaved, their seeds a little cyanide: scorpions.

CHARLIE BECKER

Making Gumbo

A good gumbo, like him
has a New Orleans skin
seamless sepia
roux
defining who
he comes from
and beneath the surface
a homegrown lexicon
like okra, the essence
of a West African bond.

Today he means
to teach her
the making of soup
as he counts and measures roots
of his Creole family tree.
She has learned
true love
begins in their kitchen
and the way to a man's heart
is through his ancestors'
cookbooks.
Heat will be passed
from his accented
Haitian words to her hands.

They begin
legs spread wide
chopping curly parsley
into fine strands
all shades of summer grass.
His muscular grip
guides the knife
precise dice of fresh celery
green bell pepper
and peels in detail
the smooth ball of yellow onion.
He sweats the tears
as his T-shirt sticks
against broad shoulders,
biceps flexed with a hunger
creamy and thick.

Their caste-iron skillet
warms to the touch
of his whisked mixture
and steady internal stir.
He breathes heavy
into the perfect pecan color
then tells her he is ready
to receive
the holy trinity.
They both stir
as minutes whirr, thyme,
cayenne pepper, Bay leaves
mingle
hand over hand in unison.

His handsome Caribbean stock
combines intimate
with boiling Louisiana water,
fleshy Andouille sausage slips
seductive
into the stainless-steel pot.
Their breaths come faster,
and deep inside
his pants pocket
pressing mighty
against an inner thigh
he touches
once, then again
a copy
of Leah Chase's
righteous recipe
for good luck.

They simmer 30 minutes
as shrimp give up
last main veins
to etiquette and the naked
force of patient fingertips.
Gulf of Mexico blue crabs
crawl into the stew
proud as Neptune
to bring it all together,
and cook for 30 minutes
while white rice waits fluffed
on the stovetop.

His full lips
wet and hungry now
ask her
if she wants
a taste.

Her tongue arches
pushing tip to teeth
and she begs him
to let her
set the table.

CLAIRE BOOKER

Bowl of Tangerines

The sweet, oily linger of late night fruit
works its devil's detail, singes
my pillow with its fire-dancing footprint.

I dream and dream of tangerines:
the soft, plump give as my thumbnail scalps.
A tint that knows how to set fire

to its own touch paper.
There's no quenching this love child
of blood and sun. Here's sky,

incendiary. Fields of Californian poppy.
Uluru's belly, gravid with sacred copper light.
A Kabuki player's rimmed eye

stares me out and zest comes
spurting down the snowy bib of my sheets
like Etna's molten lava.

Time to lassoo this bucking beast –
a shade that's got no verbal twin to heel it in.
I try revenge, falange, blancmange,

but there's no slip-knot for orange.
It twists into splinters – begins to circle slyly
through ornamental waters.

DESPY BOUTRIS

As The Day Morphs into Dusk

the girl watches the farmworkers
take off, watches them shut the gate
to the avocado grove, collects

lamb bones, sun-bleached & scattered
throughout the field. She whistles
at a bird, waits for it to return her tune.

It doesn't. So she turns, scales the gate
adorned with PRIVATE PROPERTY signs,
decides to take a souvenir or two

home with her. A year later, the man
who owns the land will hold a rifle
to her spine & then she'll never come back.

But for now, she tramps through the maze
of trees, palming & picking the fruit, ripe
& there for the taking.

CATHY BRYANT

Come Eat with Me and Be My Love

Come eat with me and be my love
and we will buy some plus size pants
and gorge on sweet syruped kisses
down supermarket food aisles dance
until thrown off the premises,
my fine eclair, my lemon puff.

Come eat with me and lose your scales
and gain lasagne, served with wine,
and ripe persimmons, plums and pears
my fragrant fruit, oh lover mine,
and we will laugh at diet cares
and low-fat bread that swiftly stales.

Come eat with me and roll on cake
and find crumbs in each other's hair
and nibble on as far as we can
until, replete, we lie quite bare
on our smooth bed of marzipan,
my love who dares to shake and bake.

Come eat with me and feel our flesh
as soft as custard, warm as toast
as comforting as treacle tart
as healthy as a hot nut roast,
my love, who nestles in my heart
- no sell-by date. Forever fresh.

Come eat with me and be my love
with chana aloo, pilau rice
with gravied pie and salted chips
and tiny pinkish sugar mice
and I'll caress your curvy hips
forever, which won't be enough.

Come eat with me. We'll dine to please;
true love is not a certain size.
Our happines is what appeals,
good appetite in both our eyes;
so let us revel in our meals
and never count the calories.

BETT BUTLER

Food Porn
in herbivorous homage to Victorian erotica

II
Sweet Potato

Sacred sacchariferous spud!
You rise from the soil like the sun ascends from the horizon.

Millennium upon millennium, paladin of the hungry
your fecund produce, undaunted by cyclone and flood
is golden manna from deep in the earth.

In Japan, you are paired with Sake
and offered to the autumnal moon
with prayers for an abundant harvest.

In America, you are boiled and mashed
shunted into a casserole
crowned by marshmallows.
Such is our folly: gilding the lily with fool's gold!

Better steamed until tender and sprinkled with salt
roasted in olive oil
or sautéed in a fragrant ablution of coconut oil and garam masala.

Better baked in your humble, threadbare jacket
oozing your caramelized lifeblood
through piercings by the sharp knife which now splits you asunder
revealing moist, sun-kissed flesh
drizzled with droplets of brown butter
and a dash of cinnamon.

O rich and flaming root!
You are the sun rising in my mouth.
I savor your blazing luminescence!

Previously published in Feathertale Review, Issue 22, December 2018.

KIRSTEN CASEY

How to Feed the Grieving

They are sensitive to cayenne, ginger, horseradish,
and prefer the bland and colorless, the texture
of gelatin, all the foods one might eat
after surgery, as the body relearns its instruction manual,
because the 10,000 taste buds on each mourner's tongue,
that muscle that helped to form the sounds of the loved one's name,
have wilted in this late frost, now gone dormant
even in spring, unable to remember
the blooming shape of each letter held in the mouth.

The shock of bright spices will stain their wooden spoons
eliminating the need for using saffron, curry, or turmeric
to enliven your sad casseroles. No amount of soaking
will remove their dye. Their vivid pigments
trigger intense reminders of memory's particular tastes.
All exotic hues mock the darkness
of their moods.

Stick to crepes, rice noodles, bone broth,
egg whites, shaved ice, soufflés—
nearly weightless cuisine that they might tolerate,
but do not crave. Stay away from the simplicity
of spreading butter, that golden constant--
wasn't it just a month ago, two chilled sticks sat
on the kitchen counter for shortbread dough, and late
in August, that last cob of white sweet corn
dripped in its greasy sunshine?
The grieving eat each day
from a calendar of tainted menus.

Get out your mandolin, slice the onions
until the slivers, translucent, almost resemble peeled
skin, cook them so long that they lose all flavor, almost
disappear. There is so much foil over Pyrex;
when they open the refrigerator door the mirrored bundles
almost reflect their long faces in the final afternoon light.
Don't make them return your dishes,
tell them to break them instead, against the patio bricks.

Remember how difficult it is to chew and sob, simultaneously:
prepare what is soft, but not soggy; do not add gruel
to their suffering. It is best not to cook anything memorable or elaborate;
pray that your dish is forgotten, pushed to the back of the freezer,
with the sanguine intention of future nourishment,
of relieving consumption.

In its abandonment, the nondescript flavors of your gesture, an attempt
at epicurean comfort, will never be associated with their tragic loss,
will be tossed out sometime next year on a fall morning
when cleaning out the fridge finally
seems like a sensible exercise, an amateur vanishing act.
Your unsavory dinner, now camouflaged in ice crystals, will come to signify
some finite healing, its disposal, an inconspicuous victory.
In Estonia, mourners serve pastries, bread, and vodka at the gravesite,
a rushed picnic of despair. Nothing comes back
with them; any food brought over a home's threshold
invites more death. Instead, they drop crusts on the dirt
for the crows, curls the birds might mistake for earthworms,
but there is no way to discern between vodka spills
and the patterns of tears trailing down the fronts of their shirts.

Consider the usefulness of leftovers,
the catharsis of saving and then wasting,
and how one day this might lead to the click of a gas burner
igniting under a copper saucepan, the first hour of a returning appetite.
Do not underestimate your simple offering: following a recipe,
and then, delivery.

GABRIEL CLEVELAND

How to Savor an Avocado

With your hands,
cradle its fullness and its weight;
press the ridges of your fingerprints
against its small, black bumps
as it gives itself, but slightly,
into your grip.
Twist the stem for a green peek within,
then halve it:
crescent movement of your knife;
hold the fruit along its newfound seam
and repeat your cut for quarters
to unfold, lotus-like,
from its tender, wooden heart.
Pinch the corner of the skin
and peel slowly, unsealing an envelope;
thumb at rest in the concave
of its verdant flesh,
two fingers arched along its back.
Welcome it to your mouth: the secret
you repeat upon first hearing
until it's part of you;
introduce it to each of your teeth,
let it swaddle the enamel
before it ever meets your throat;
like desperately good news, swallow
slowly, so it will last.

TERENCE CULLETON

Bone

The way the sprawled dog gnawed
a T-bone all day, tugging gristle, grinding
at a marbly spur, shellacking fissures
with her long, loving tongue — her passion
staring at floorboards
as at a vision of marrow, the way
her ears bounced when she raked a groove,
mouth straining down
in an ecstatic grimace — the fact
she was manic with little more
than the idea of meat, its memory,
a greasy trace in a crack, a gnarled
fleck on a nub — her deep love for it,
her belief in it, like a theory one gives
one's life to without adding costs:
rabbits unchased, holes
not dug. The way she lay back
at last, uncognizant, serene, bone
discarded like some lacy underthing
on the bordello floor of her lustings:
that's how you and I should live.

Previously published in The Schuylkill Valley Journal, Volume 28, Spring 2009.

Cooking

Don't remember my mother ever smiling
as she cooked our nightly meals. There was
always the cigarette, and the glass of red wine,
her hair tied up in a bun, most nights barefoot
on the linoleum, most nights she'd sway to the
music of my youth, the Bee Gees or Fleetwood
Mac, but I never saw her smile through a
thousand hamburger helpers or lasagna or
ham steaks, but she must have, right?
Each night she'd fill our plates, bellies,
even our souls, with nourishment. So tell
me how it's possible that couldn't have
brought her even a little bit of joy?

JOHN DAVIS

Desire

As much as I love life
I love blackberry pie
a la mode even more
heavy on the mode

Yes that slice
bubbling over and the mode
dripping down from a crust
so flaky smooth

it could calm
any terrorist
into shaking hands
with enemies

And when at last
they cremate me
under a sun
as rich as honey

place a pie
in that crematorium
Let me enter the next world
with blackberries on my lips

JOHN DORROH

Pepper Marriage

I've fallen in love with hot stuff.
I've let ketchup lag behind with its cliffs
of sugar, its white crystals clogging up the
highways and roads. I've graduated from
5000 Scovilles of serranos and sissy
jalapeno, to the 40,000 tongue-curling
heat units of Aji Amarillo, pequin, and Tobsaco.
Heat makes me move fast like a man on fire
who needs to jump in a cold lake. My taste buds
are numb and wait for reconditioning. It sometimes
takes an hour for the pain too pass into euphoria
like what I just did to myself. Again. I am captivated
by capsaicin, mesmerized by its grip, its talismanic
gumption to jump out of a bowl of New Mexico
chili into thousands of dishes in so many cultures
where even the children end up wanting more.

JENNIFER EDWARDS

Father's Grapefruit

Westerns seeped in while he traced the curves,
crafted swift but tender separations of fruit and skin.
    Strong-armed business suit slice down the middle,
    glottal stop of steel meeting battered board.
        Back bent as the monogrammed r on his
        handkerchiefs below the beige cupboards.

With him, breakfast was never cereal or eggs; nothing without
a proper season or seal, like those disks crystalized overnight.
    When we woke, we found bright yellow oceans,
    sugar slick as ice (I loved to watch him cut through that, too).

He was gone while we savored our sweet suns. Mother orbited
her familiar Formica, her coffee cold and dark as a saddle,
    always reaching with her slightly open robe
    casting shadows on crustless dry bread.

Previously published in Unsymmetrical Body (Finishing Line Press, 2022).

LINDA McCAULEY FREEMAN

Dinner with My Ex at the Lucky Noodle

Both elbows of your plaid shirt—another I've never
seen—are on the table as you reach for the fried

noodles, dip them in duck sauce, crunch them whole
and you are laughing—those perfect white teeth

belying the photograph your orthodontist once showed
me of you at 12—your mouth an overcrowded city—

I think: *How young you still look.* And of the time
at the Stormville Flea Market when a vendor

asked you if your mother wanted to buy his books
and I realized he meant me. Your eyes are green today,

because of the shirt—I always loved that about your eyes
until even color did them no good. We trade stories

stack them side by side like our two old
blue teacups that each had a crack running

from the rim. I look for the crack in your words,
the pain of living without me. Then you tell me

about her—or rather about you and her,
since I've known her as long as you have—

the little goo-goo-eyed girl, now grown,
younger sister of one of my bridesmaids.

You say she's jealous of the 18-year-old girl
on your job: "I swear, Lin, she looks like you,

only you're prettier. "And how hard it is for you.
But I'm stuck on *you're prettier* and I want to shout

When did you think I was pretty? And reroll our history
to that moment and return there with you.

Previously published in Trailer Park Quarterly, 2020.

KATHERINE GAFFNEY

Manners at the Table: How to Eat a Lobster—Boiled or Broiled
After Amy Vanderbilt

The body will beckon you
on the pristine plate before
you, carmine and muscular.
Approach the plate as you
might a frightened, living
thing: with the left hand,
press its torso to the plate,
as if fixing unruly tendrils
of hair, twist the crustacean's
claws off with your right
hand, affix the pincers
to your plate's lip like you
might ornaments on a wreath.
Lift the tail's cloud-meat
and slice into bite-sized
segments, spear a piece
with your fork, right hand
of course, and dip into melted
butter or mayonnaise as you dip
yourself into the sea to glisten
with salt. Return to the small
claws pouring from the animals'
torso like a many-armed god
and gently suck the meat
from each length's severed
end. Adjust your cheeks,
to accommodate for your own
considerations as to how this will
be received. With the U of a nut
cracker take the claws waiting
for you on the plate and pluck
the meat from the skeletal frame
as you might have fished

for the matching earring you wore
tonight from your jewelry box,
dip in butter or mayonnaise.
With seafood fork, ferry the rest
of the meat deemed worthy
to your mouth, do not leave
the green liver or scarlet roe
(depending on whether you
have been served male or female).
As a spectacle of true lobster
love you will unhinge the lobster's
back to open the body, much
as you open yours when you
unclasp your bra at day's end.
Capture the remaining sweet
morsels from this excavated body.

REUVEN GOLDFARB

Living Off the Land Around the Bay

Fennel growing in the vacant lots
and chamomile growing in the sidewalk cracks;
white wine in a clear plastic cup left out
on the brick wall that protects a garden
in Pacific Heights, after a party;
ripe blackberries plucked from thorny brambles;
baked potatoes and pizza crusts exhumed
from the trash on Telegraph Avenue;
discarded vegetables selected
from the overflowing Co-op refuse bin;
the store's free samples, offered with a smile;
a piece of bread the baker gives when asked;
the tender cherry plums on Essex Street;
lamb's tongue and mustard greens from the fields;
miner's lettuce near the shady park creek;
windfall apples from the crossroads orchard;
wrinkled pears clustered along a fence,
on a country road, in a time of drought
— all these and more, to be savored and enjoyed —
manna born of earth, rain, and seed,
human labor and nature's fecundity,
more than enough to feed this tramp.

ERICA GOSS

Dinner at Manresa

Our table awaited us, lit with droplets of phosphorescent seawater,
each napkin wrapped, tucked and tied with stems of Neolithic rye.

We began with a salad of sea vegetables harvested by unmarried mermen
and wedges of cheese from cows fed white flowers in moonlight.

A few hours later our waiter brought the voice of the west wind
caught in hinged bamboo boxes, then a bonsai forest sculpted from

iced asparagus, arranged in terrariums, and drizzled with dewberry sauce,
followed by dark brown breasts of Muscovy duck trimmed in silver feathers

and dappled with salted foam – our knives touched – too much?
My fork tapped the slope of a miniature mountain amended

with live mushrooms, nestled on a plate of scented grasses,
undulating in the warm breeze. For dessert, the view from 30,000 feet

rendered in clouds of meringue, and a small box to open later which
we held in our interlaced fingers like the promise we made all those years
ago.

Previously published in Annapurna, Fall 2014 issue.

CONNIE JORDAN GREEN

An Ode to Figs in August

This tear-drop droop of sweetness
encased in tawny skin, golden skin,
purple-hued skin—Brown Turkey,
Celeste, Black Mission—this perfect
bite of summer ripeness, this bundle
of sun, rain, long days come to fruition,
this laden fig tree trimmed with its own
ornaments, and, oh, the lights—like
starburst come to rest on our lips,
like the first sip of well-aged burgundy
sliding over our tongues, caressing
the palate, come to restore our souls.

GEORGE GUIDA

Bourdain Said

"Bourdain said," my mother said as though he were
her devil, my mother, confined to a chair by years of toil
for others, like Bourdain in his kitchen or on the road
in places my mother had never been and sure as hell
would never get to now. Bourdain spoke to her
from Rio de Janeiro, Istanbul, Bangkok, Lagos.

She'd found her man, unafraid to risk his life
for a hearty meal. He rolled through Yaba,
asking the locals to smother his moi moi and fufu
until he kissed them and asked them to dance
at the club where my mother let it all hang out,
getting low to the Afrobeat and nibbling his ear.

There was my mother, ageless, arm in arm with him
strolling down the Avenida Atlântic
claiming an oceanfront bench, to share
a bowl of bobó de camarão and a caipirinha
just as the night breeze cooled the coast, her head
on his blousy shoulder, dissolving in the mist.

Previously published in The Daily Drunk, September 2021.

MRINALINI HARCHANDRAI

Kitchen Konkani

My mother married Bombay
her Konkan palate
spoke a tongue
out of place
in our Sindhi jawlines
she gave them to me
when she bantered
with our Karwar fingered cook
about how to make the curry
taste like her Panjim kitchen
in the pot
dried red chillies swam
like crocodiles
with territorial bite
I learnt to smack my lips
with useful words

like compliments
"jevonk borey"
you have good taste
because it is delicious

and to ham
"bhoroun di!"
do you want me to starve?
fill up the plate then!

I learnt to compromise on colas
"Okay, ordhem Thums Up aata, ordhem magir"
half now, half later

I learnt recipe secrets
"kitkem naal galta"
the precision of coconutiness

I learnt body parts
like the eyes – "dollé"
the first organ to ingest food

I learnt about the seasons
of less salt
"meet komi zalem"

I learnt vegetables
"bhendé, gosai ani karate"
to pick out the unappetizing ones

and I learn that I am in a pickle
"bezar korum naka, chol!"
when she said,
"Don't eat my head!"

Notes

Konkani: A language born from the mix of Portuguese and Marathi, spoken by population along the Konkan coast of west India.
Jevonk borey: Konkani for "the food is delicious".
Bhorun di: Konkani for "fill it up".
Ordhem aata, ordhem magir: Konkani for "half now, half later".
Kitkem naal galta: Konkani for "how much coconut to be used?"
Dollé: Konkani for "eyes".
Meet komi zalem: Konkani for "the salt is less".
Bhende: Konkani for "okra".
Gosai: Konkani for "ridge gourd".
Karaate: Konkani for "bitter gourd".

Excerpted from A Bombay in my Beat, Mrinalini Harchandrai (Bombaykala Books, 2nd ed. 2018).

J. DAVID HARPER

In the Checkout Line at Trader Joe's

In the corner of our basket
between the bread and the apples
is a bottle of wine
we picked because
we liked the label.

It is a staple
like oatmeal and potatoes
because we both know
though neither of us says so
it's not really a bottle of wine.

It's a promise we make
that no matter where we go
or what we do
this week we'll end up together
and our glasses will be full.

MUREALL HEBERT

The Liberation of Sunlight and Hope

We made jam in the kitchen,
the windows   flung wide
to let in a non-existent breeze.
       My mother said stir, so I stirred
as seeds swam in pools
of raspberry juice,   forbidden
and heady, like the menstrual blood I had
yet to bleed but coveted the way
a pupa pines metamorphosis.
       As the jars cooled,
canning lids popped   and my mother said,
     that'll be you one day,
a lid snapping shut   on a heavenly union
       of fresh wildness and sugar.
You'll blend into perfection and sit
on a shelf where you'll   wait
to be opened, scooped out,
and spread   on rustic bread.
       Perhaps you'll be cherished
like a bottle of fine wine drawing legs
down the sides of a glass.
       Or maybe you'll hide
     on a shelf forever,
gathering dust,   forgotten,
the way preserved goods sometimes do.
       I considered her carefully,
trying to see the jam inside her.
Was she strawberry? Marmalade? Fine wine?
Were her seeds   hard nuggets   of longing?
      I   would never sit on a shelf,
never let myself be   scooped out.
      I   would do the spreading,
the opening,   like the carnal folds

of the iris flower, fingertips stroking petals.
My seeds would surface, stripped bare.
      Later that night,
I snuck down to the kitchen, unsealed each jar,
      and let the berry scent
seduce me. Spoon in hand,
      I ate and ate and ate,
each drop sliding   over my tongue
as raspberry kisses stained
my lips.

Previously published in Qu.

EMILY HOCKADAY

Seasonal Diet

In quarantine I think about Rainier cherries. In Chinatown
they sell them 1.99/lb. The big metal scoops are just
for show—the yellow and pink flesh too prone to bruising
are instead lovingly hauled by hand to the hanging scales.
Even nine months pregnant, sweating and in compression
socks, I walked up Broadway
to return with bright red bags brimming.
My husband would bring me five pounds at a time.
Their season is just around the corner. My daughter
learned to love them, too. The pucker, the sugar,
the ping of the pit as it hits a ceramic bowl. The juice
and the blush of the thin skin. We are lucky;
I know it. We work and share childcare.
Our paychecks still come. Our daughter
is not not okay. Food fills our kitchen. I am selfish
to still think about the cherries. Will they rot
in the branches? Will the workers be kept safe
and distant? Will they ship to stores I'm too scared
to shop in? Will they taste the same, without
the pavement pounding, the salt on my upper lip,
the pink cheeks from my lunch hour walk, with no sunblock?

Previously published in Poets Reading the News.

KAREN PAUL HOLMES

Macedonian Bean Soup

I used to pass the Heavenly Ham shop,
think of the bean soup
Father taught my ex to make
and see them in our kitchen
chopping yellow onions just so,
the secret pinch of mint,
peppers a little too hot for me
but not for them,
how of all the sons-in-law
he was the one who asked to learn,
how I would never have his soup again.

That sadness—some said
it would linger, that my cheerful self
would have a chink.
It would add character.

These years later, the leaving
has become a blessing.
I read my ex's tomato-splashed
notes, but it's Father's accent I hear
and the sizzle of ham hocks browning.

Beans and broth stew in my Le Creuset
with peppers from a local farm.
I've settled my bones at the shore
of a silver-blue lake,
where mountains echo fireworks
on the Fourth of July,
chinks of brilliance in a black sky.

Previously published in a slightly different form in No Such Thing as Distance by Karen Paul Holmes (Terrapin Books, 2018). The recipe for this soup is also in the book.

JOHN HOPPENTHALER

Ghirardelli: San Francisco

*"Studies show women crave chocolate
more than any other food"
—newspaper clipping*

At the start of the 17th century, pious
Mexican women sipped hot chocolate in church

Bittersweet warmth filled their earthly bodies,

& their spirits levitated above the cloistered
drone of mass. In their eyes, the transported
glassiness of sexual gratification. Jealous

of such passion, the bishop forbade the practice.
His imminent death was bliss, poison slipped
into his own bowl of cocoa before matins.

Montezuma thought it an aphrodisiac & quaffed
dozens of goblets a day. Bronze & doomed,
in the throes of ecstasy he'd picture the certain

swoop & rise of condors behind the shut
wings of his eyelids. At Fisherman's Wharf,
I buy a sampler box for Valentine's Day,

anticipate your teeth marks on every piece.
The one shaped & grooved like a seashell
might cause you to grow unpredictable

as the Pacific. Inside the perfect, dark square,
the tropical swell of coconut or oh, please,
yes sugar drift of caramel. Will you place

a wafer laced with praline on my tongue?
Back from a New World, I'll come like Columbus
to Fernando's court & offer the innocent gift.

MARY LOUISE KIERNAN

Perugian Pear

Perugian
Pear
To call it
simply a drupe,
the botanical label
bestowed upon stone fruits,
is to know neither the vision of
its triple layers of skin, stone, & flesh,
nor the hidden kernel at the center of this
alabaster pear graced by one verdigris leaf
with polished streaks its loving sculptor
would refer to as "stains of berry blue,"
nor as an object of art presented
sweetly by its object of
affection.

EMILEE KINNEY

Ode to the Fish-Fry

We arrived like the fish did   barreled in truck beds
        swaying with backroad drifts and fishtails coughing dust ducking rocks
            and holding onto each other for dear life.

The driver: step- father, their father, man who loved my mother.
We: little sister, me, and step- sisters, step- brother.
        The family I had always wanted, but didn't know I was about to lose
like the fish

snatched up out of the creek, out of the lake,   unexpecting

now outside sizzling in fryers, their discarded scales and spines crimsoning softened snow.

Somewhere, the chainsaw whine of snowmobiles
        and their headlights pulsing through trees,
desperate to hold onto winter.

        Our hair, stiff and windblown, now sags with the heavy heat
        of bodies and grease as we join the rest of the village filling
        this barn packed with too much food, rusted folding chairs,
        and coolers of Bud and Jack scattered like dice.

Wooden walls wet with olive oil
        dripping in beads   coating taxidermy heads in glossy tears

cigarette, wood smoke, cooking steam:
        a dense haze we breathe and dance through
        as a southern twang none of us can mimic swings from the rafters'
                zip-tied speakers.

Tables bow with stacks of fried pickles, crusted green beans,
crispy corn, crowns of golden cod, and the squelch of cold macaroni
salad quickly warming. On my sister's plate, a greased aspen leaf she begged them
to fry for her.

The only memories I have of my mother's laugh
        are in this place of food and sweat and lime-flavored beer
her head tossed back, strawberry-blond shining in mason-jar light
        her arm falling easy across stepdad's shoulders, his working hands on her thigh

            I wish I would have held onto that sound
                more than I worried about the fish yet to be fried, slick and stinking
                    in metal buckets, floating atop melted ice. And like the rest of us:
                                    dead-eyed and dancing.

PHYLLIS KLEIN

Cultivation

The yellow lacy-edged squash, green beans, sweet peas,
broccolini. Arugula, baby red-leaf lettuce, all organic,

each of these in my vegetable box, in my frying pan,
on the table, fruits of the dirt picked from their plants,

children weaned from mothers' wombs. Fields
at midnight when laborers arrive, knives, gloves, baseball caps,

half asleep from journeys to cross borders or follow
the harvest as bushes prepare their offspring in ripening.

Everything so fragile, so transient, fields almost ready
to be stripped again, plowed into submission, another growing season.

Workers, bent at the back to meet their livelihood, to feed
the people. And now, not only the jeopardy of deportation,

also infected air, hidden danger in their fellow
workers' breath, and, as if the food was meant

to cook right on its vine. The ease of spoilage.
Does the harvester begin to hate the beautiful,

perfect progeny, sensuous cabbage, proud okra?
Could he never bear to eat again another translucent lettuce leaf,

another holy stalk of kale? Grind of muscle, stretched over
vertebrae for a wage low enough to keep him worried, exhausted.

Boxes brought to my door, perfectly packed. No toxic smoke, no
taste of regret or disappointment on their sturdy vegetable bodies,

rejoicing in the glow of existence, newly delivered. Let no one be hungry.
Let me bow to backs that bent at the hip to reach the carrots,

hands that held knives to cut broccoli, hearts that persevered
next to the beat of harvester machines, rhythms of feeding.

J.I. KLEINBERG

Pieces of Silver

I wonder how it is to be a spoon. To slip one curve
beneath, to gentle from its bowl a berry, slide edge-wise
into ice cream, into the warm cavern of a mouth.
How it is to both resist and hold flavor in the declension
of the body, to separate and deliver, to stir in clinking dance.
Friend to hand and tongue, to absinthe, to dish —
remember the cow? remember the moon?

Dulled-edged, round-toothed knives school in the drawer,
silvery herring, decorous for butter and condiments,
honey and peas, familiars to plate and tablecloth.
I wonder how it is to be a real blade — remember the mice?
— honed to hurt, to shear, stab, cleave. How it is to slice,
paper-thin, a gift for the tongue: fresh tomato, ripe peach.
How it is to be fanged, incisive, to be a surgeon for the truth.

How far we are now from nursery rhyme, from spooning
in the velvet-lined night. Implement taunts us, stainless
both praise and accusation. Forklift, pitchfork, runcible spoon.
The drawer turned upside down, tarnished words noisy and futile.
Emily Post cannot resolve this clattered escalation of utensils.
Switchblade, forked tongue. What price a place at the table?

MIRIAM KOTZIN

Only a Lady Poet

would write about
asparagus,
thumb-thick, thrusting
almost visibly up
through yielding earth.

Reader, you have
a dirty mind.
I simply meant
a growing crop,
each stalk rising
from a tangle of roots.

Or bunched,
bundled bound
by a rubber band,
trimmed and loosed
into a pan, simmering.

Most are erect,
but others condescend,
incline their heads
towards others as at any
cocktail party.

No gentleman poet
would write about
asparagus; gentlemen
poets grow visibly
famous writing
about, say, plums.

MARK L. LEVINSON

Carrots

Floating in dark earth, each carrot believes

it is the only carrot in the world.

There must be someone, though, who sees them all,

row upon row, patient as fresh candles.

Could they be innocent of time? Or do they count

the instances of breeze that touch them from

the ineffable ghostly dimension

into which their feeble plumes protrude?

There must be someone who can see them all,

the whole buried sculpted army of them,

someone— who does know time: icicle time,

stalactite time, the thunder of harvest--

watching through a subterranean lens,

or why else would the carrots be orange?

RAYMOND LUCZAK

Uvulae

Our mouths are born to sin.
We should know better than to gulp

down 32 ounces of sugared water
but damn, there's something unredeemable

about those endless highways of
nowhere paved over with bitterness

that drive us to seek solace in places
where no church can save us.

We shouldn't be stuffing those alms
of perfectly layered potato chips

laced with the sodium of addiction
into our mouths. Asking for help is hard.

We shouldn't be grateful for such dirty shame,
but our souls are gluttons for redemption.

Previously published in the Mid-Atlantic Review.

LINDA MALNACK

Moussaka

When I think mother, I think moussaka,
the best of 100 best hamburger dishes
of 1965. I remember mother rubbing
the meat between her fingers, dropping it
into the electric pan and the sound it made,
louder and louder, like a crowd cheering.
I remember potatoes peeled and precisely
cubed, canned tomatoes, whole, she mashed
with the back of a fork, the splash of red
cooking wine, and bay leaves floating
above the bubble and splash before the lid
came down. And the smell of it, a fusion
of wine and tomatoes, beef and potatoes,
and the taste, the taste. But better than that,
the word moussaka, the way it conjured
a place warmer and more welcoming than
winters south of Buffalo, where often snow
drifted against the house like massive
white domes and the sky burned Aegean.

JOHN C. MANNONE

I Love You More Than Popcorn

There's a pearly translucence to the kernels of corn,
whose hulls hold a hardened starch, which catch the
glints of kitchen light. Shimmers in hot bacon grease
remain hidden when the lid of a cast iron kettle-pan
shuts tight. But the glint in your grandfather's eyes
will linger there, for a while, in that prolonged light

      of your memory. Pangs. From inside

the endosperm, superheated steam pings the popped
corn against the metal cover, it triggers your agitation
of the pan—a methodical turning of the handle
driving metal fins shaped like boat propeller blades
to scrape kernels off the bottom of the gas-fired pot
keeping them from scorching while lifting up
the foamed white puffs of starch. You anticipate
the taste, the crunch, and you carefully control these
explosions just like your grandfather taught you.

      No wonder you love popcorn so much,
      he was the only one who understood
      your desperate hunger, your craving
      for the kind words your mother never knew
      how to speak to you when you were five,
      and even now, often burnt and bitter.

You'd think that your mother's popcorn pan,
fitted with a pressure relief valve, would make
great popcorn, but she shuffled the round-bottom
pot over electric burners too hard too long
and wore the metal thin. It was always low yield.

After you learned how in first grade, you wrote
a letter to your grandfather with large printed words
puffed-up, saying that if you took the bus to his house,
you hoped that he would pick you up and let you live
with him. He kept your letter in his wallet, together
with his smiles for years. Maybe it was his popcorn.

Only your grandfather's popcorn, and maybe even
mine with a hint of sea salt and butter on my lips
pressed to yours, can satisfy. You said you love me
more than popcorn… I took your hand and kissed it,
then said the kindest words that I could think of,
Let's go to the movies… And you understood.

Previously published in The Ekphrastic Review, September issue, 2018.

KAREN GREENBAUM-MAYA

BLAT

Not salad, fries, he said,
and the BLT,
on white, toasted, extra mayo,
and make it a BLAT
and I'll take a real Coke
and why not?
for he'd no need now
to stave off pleasure
to save up for old age
having reached eighty-nine
and just left the oncologist's office
where they told us
about the metastases
and the nodes
and the mass.

MICHAEL MINGO

On First Eating Crawfish

Right as I tear the specimen apart,

a stream of seasoned juices cascades down
my fingers, palms, arms. Once again, my form

is too indelicate. Denied the joy
of sucking out the ocean from its head,
that shot of brackish water I embrace

after it passes, I turn my energies
to the top ring of shell, the one that keeps

the tail from my lips. Fumbling to find

the weakness in its armor, some gap to force
its body open, my thumbs get stained with dye

crushed from the shell. I'm guilty of impatience.
Best to proceed as slowly as my grandma
unfolding wrapping paper creases, bent

on saving every scrap for next year's gifts.
A little twist, the lightest tug—it's free.

I bite into the meat, pinch from the bottom,

swallow. So little fruit for so much effort,
and only when the taste of iron swells

like the flood tide somewhere along the Gulf
does the brute fact some unseen shard has sliced
open my lower lip occur to me:

one last, belated act of self-defense.
As if the fool who labored on this puzzle

would think the threat of blood sufficient warning.

THOMAS MIXON

Compulsorily Wholesome

Fuji some, then Fuji more.
Four bites first of broccoli.
Even when covered with cheese,
the child hopes we'll forget
the count, fork over slices
before the persistent veg.
We tend to get specific

with red fruit, with yummy things.
We find the missing vowel
behind the couch. We spell out
nutritive requirements.
The letters let us lettuce
dinner with limited words.
The child deserves dessert.

WILDA MORRIS

In Defense of the Apricot

*. . . apricots make
disappointing peaches....
~ Terese Svoboda*

The peach is the sun
perched precariously on the horizon
Listen closely, it sounds like fire
(or wind shaking peach trees
and blowing a wayward newspaper
up Main Street)
or the dove humming its lament
on the fireplace chimney
Apricots sound like the children's choir
at vespers, rich and sweet
songs dripping down your chin
The apricot is the full moon,
the blood moon the jaguar hungers for
but can't reach

JILL MUNRO

Don't Bring the Turkey to the Table,

he said that Christmas his veggie girlfriend
came for dinner, she won't be able to stomach it whole.
I had visions of a girl bird-mouth open

swallowing kilos of plucked flesh
free-range-roasted-skin-legs-thighs-breast
wings-wishbone-stuffing and all.

I didn't bring it to the table, I kitchen-carved it,
sliced white meat and dark, disguised with giblet
gravy, the carcass of a gobbling, strutting

feathers gleaming, red wattle-wobbling
living bird, sawn, plated for the carnivores.
Nobody minded the pigs-in-blankets,

nestling undercover by the electric green
of leftover, bitter sprouts.

SHARON LASK MUNSON

Friday Afternoon at Mahane Yehuda Marketplace

The *Shuk* in the center of downtown Jerusalem
pulsates with shoppers and vendors.

Merchants offer samples of buttery sesame halvah,
morsels of cinnamon rugelach,
choice bits of Turkish and Kurdish sweets:
baklava, marzipan, rice pudding.

Inside the bustling open-air market
locals and tourists pack lanes
leading to narrow stalls
and a bewildering array of goods—

jars of oil, barrels of olives,
sheep's milk cheeses,
almonds, hundreds of spices,
fresh citrus, oven-baked pita, challah.

In the Iraqi section,
behind falafel stands and juice bars,
old men play backgammon, cards,
slouch at wooden tables,
sip from tiny cups of espresso.

Hasidic Jews in dark three-piece suits
crowned by black hats of rabbit fur
shop alongside Sabras
in skimpy jeans and sandals.

Shopkeepers fill cloth bags with fish, beef, fowl,
dates, figs, peppers, potatoes, lamb,
braided breads, almond cakes,
thick white Sabbath candles, sunflowers—
stocking up for Shabbat.

A young, pink-cheeked member
of the Israeli Defense Forces,
Uzi over his right shoulder,
stands guard at the entrance off Jaffa Street

clutching in his suntanned hand
one double dip, pistachio ice cream cone
dusted with sprinkles.

RUSSELL NICHOLS

Closed Mouths Don't Get Fed

closed mouths don't get fed, mama
   said, but fed mouths don't stay hungry.
   can't forget those loud days my tummy
taught my spirit how to rumble; trauma

comes from lifetimes between meals,
   but i know better than to wait for good
   service; the catch du jour is the hood
with special "eat-'em-alive!" deals.

here, souls get lost like appetites;
   prayers to-go for the sick and shut-in
   from hypocrites who dish on gluttons,
but feast their eyes via satellites.

hunger—strikes three times against us.
   unlevel playing field where kneeling
   is the new sit-in; audibles for healing
get you sacked for being conscientious.

but i chew on leftover rules you taught
   four-hundred times to break it down.
   closed mouths don't make a sound,
so i spit out loud this food for thought.

ARLENE PLEVIN

Blackberries

I did not ask
the blackberries to come
over the hedge
to my side.
They hang full lipped
dark, like seeded eyes,
dark, a clot of fruit,
spider webs glistening nearby,
threads of light.

I did not ask
the blackberries to fall
against the house,
staining the wood,
black thumbprints,
no, almost purple.
A purple so royal
that kings & queens would run
for their plumpness
give up kingdoms & fiefdoms
for a scoop.

KYLE POTVIN

Ramps

Poached Eggs on Toast with Ramps
—Bon Appétit

Hail young allium!
Spring onion,
wild leek.

Your season is brief
yet you are complicated,
three parts in one:
pungent bulb that hides
beneath the surface, magenta stem,
broad tender leaf that disappears by summer.

Your ancestors have lined rivers
and fed tribes.
A city—Chicagou—
is named in your honor!

Some try to preserve you,
pickle you,
for the months ahead
but I say:

Sizzle in the heat of the pan.
Soften to unexpected sweetness.
Join with the delicate egg, poached,
on a thick slice of toast,
thinly spread with cheese:
fresh goat, ricotta, burrata.

This Sunday morning,
rock the Maldon.
Run with the abandon
of broken yolk.

Previously published in Eat This Poem (Oct. 2016) and in Loosen (Hobblebush Books, 2021).

CLAUDIA M. REDER

How to Braid Challah

I. Ingredients
You will be baking
with languages.
Russian, German,
and Yiddish
will suffice-
but contain
large quantities
of gluten—

II. Mixing the Dough
While you
knead the flour and yeast,
gathering strength
in your arms
and volume
in your voice!
Such heated
discussions
until the children
scream, Stop arguing!
and you retort
we are not arguing.
We are discussing
Aunt Ruthie
and your lost tooth
and Rachel's
report card
and Zena's last
doctor's appointment
for TMJ
slap slapping down
turn turning it over

in the dough--
your conversations
rise, conflate.

III. Cutting and Braiding
Don't forget to flour
the board every so often--
sweeping your hand
across the marble,
a clean slate.

IV. Optional
Brush with egg
white twice
so the loaves glisten-
once after
braiding
and again after
baking
in honor
of your
Russian
grandmother
who threw two
kisses, one
for each cheek;
or sprinkle
a Yinglish
of raisins,
or poppy seeds.

V. Serving the Challah
Invite oodles of people.
Tear off chunks.
Dance with your bread.
Let the crumbs
fall on the good table
       cloth, so be it.

Previously published in Lilith, summer 2009 and in How to Disappear (Blue Light Press, 2019).

LISA REYNOLDS

Nana Loves to Eat Strawberries

She slips out at dawn
in her nightdress
leaves foot prints
in dew rich grass
towards a trellis
covered in vines
while I watch
from a window
as she plucks
a red shaped heart
and brings it to her lips

THOMAS RICHARDSON

And All God's People Said "Amen"

When my grandmother died,
the preacher eulogized her coconut cake.
Somewhere between "Psalm 23" and "Blessed Assurance,"
he gave those packed in the pews at
Manly Presbyterian Church
a revival in confectioner's sugar and full-fat milk.
While the Hammond warbled behind him,
the Reverend Doctor picked up speed,
wiped his brow as he reminded every mourner
that the only grace there was
was the grace they could taste,
the kind that paints a sheen on the lips,
and in Etta's kitchen, there was a slice for every
widow, orphan, outcast, and addict.
Into your hands we commend your sweet servant, Lord.
What is love but four sticks of butter, hand whipped
and spread smooth behind an unlatched screen door?

Previously published in Intégrité and in How to Read (Friendly City Books, 2021).

KAREN RIGBY

Pistachios

Crushing mint-green
meat for the white bowl

of ice cream, picture
Iranian trees ripening

in August. A valley
of hands. How a hectare

rings. Think of sea
green bottle shards.

Nebuchadnezzar's
garden swept clean

of detritus. Paper
funnels torn length-

wise. Red dye.
Cousin to cashews,

but more prized.
Salt seed for larders.

Buy rosewater vials.
Pair with blood orange

or crush in baklava.
Hull pistachios

to their sweet engines.
From San Joaquin Valley

to the Silk Road, bloom
deserts on your tongue.

KIM ROBERTS

Pantoum with Catheter and Total Parenteral Nutrition

The uneaten food in the fridge
was more symbol than sustenance,
but she simply couldn't throw it out.
Her body was pocked with tubes.

More symbol than sustenance—
the spice rack, the cookbooks—
although her body was pocked with tubes
and her food was a thick yellow liquid.

The spice rack, the cookbooks,
the years of kitchen lore:
now her food was a thick yellow liquid
dripping through her IV.

The years of kitchen lore
were one identity sloughed off.
Dripping through her IV:
her past, reduced like a sauce.

One identity sloughed off,
the food uneaten in the fridge
was her past, ashen, reduced—
and she simply couldn't throw it out.

Whiskey

I need whiskey to help me
write this poem.

Not because I spoke to the dead today
or because my feet squished inside my wet

sneakers and rain dribbled down my neck.
Not because I worried when I couldn't find

Chuck at our meeting spot even though he
rode ahead of me and should have arrived

first. Not because I said goodbye to the
prayer tree and Galway Bay and our

renovated thatched roof cottage. Not
because I ate crumble laced with rhubarb

grown on this island or because I met
Gabriel who taught me how to make

goat cheese or because I finally
found a fisherman who would sell me

fish and I had to say no because
I already had pork chops at home

and it was my last night here to cook.
Not because I felt like Diedre's thirty-seven

cousins were now my family or because
the wind was singing in our chimney.

It's like Diane saying when you drink
whiskey it's time to play cards

or maybe she said when you play
cards it's time to drink whiskey.

Either way, one
plus one equals two.

ELLEN SAZZMAN

Lemon: An Essence

Tell me, what is one? What is laymun, leman,
  limon, limone, constant cognate

among Anglo-Saxon, Semitic, Latinate?
  Tongues of sun and moonlight fill spaces

between leaves, stars, fruit plucked from
  the knowledge tree shimmering with juices

to purify the root of a palate, the palette
  of Turner's lemon-infused skies, storm omens.

Sour sweetness puckers lips into a kiss to be
  planted – the savior of apples, avocadoes, the soul.

The flower of memory, Proust's madeleine dipped in
  lemon tea, infuses the bouquet of maternal embrace.

Lazarus' rigid hand conceals the etrog's rind.
  His jaundiced flesh absorbs its unbared scent.

Do Father's fists still grip the wheel of his '57 two-toned
  aqua/chrome Ford Edsel, the one he called his lemon?

Previously published in The Shomer (Finishing Line Press, 2021).

CARLA SCHWARTZ

Chicken of the Woods

Just this morning, I said this would not be the year for them—
I'd been walking and looking, but just as the acorn
hides under leaf, they had eluded me.

Later, picking my way through the raspberries I'd neglected all week,
wedged into the old honey locust stump in the middle of the patch,
I saw them—pillows the color of candy corn fanning from the wood.

Before that, I had given up—one more reason to sell the house—
but just seeing the yellows and oranges—colors so bright
they looked fake—convinces me to stay.

We will not poison you, they say, we are spongy and meaty—not candy.
We won't take you on a trip, or give you bad dreams,
but leave some of us behind, so we'll return to feed you again.

Tucked into the wood seams of the old stump,
the thin fingers of mushroom I hadn't severed, remain—
the pale pink flesh, firm and rubbery.

I like how, thinly sliced and sautéed,
the mushrooms surrender their brightness—
the oranges dull to a color akin to the dark meat of chicken.

I suck at the bulb of red blooming on my finger
where I'd cut more than mushroom from the trunk.
I dip a fork into the pan to taste, hoping I didn't cut off too much.

MISTEE ST. CLAIR

Singing the Willamette Valley

I.
We harvest the figs
while your husband grills chicken and ribs,
summer squash and new potatoes.
The figs are just splitting,
a clear juice dripping and sticking
to our hands as we tug and tear
them from the tree.
They are best spongy soft,
overripe, the green teardrop orbs
heavy with a clear, liquid gold.
It's a mad, daily gathering,
to pick each in its exquisiteness,
so that few fall to the ground.
Though none are wasted
from the dog's daily inspection.
And then, there is the eating of figs.
This night, dessert: stuffed with goat cheese,
wrapped in prosciutto,
drizzled with balsamic and grilled.
How easy it is to bask in this gluttony,
swilling the summer,
eager for the next drop.

II.
Blackberries stained into our fingertips
like purple kisses. It is hot and the beer is cold.
In your garden, small orange tomatoes plump,
sweet as gumdrops. The boys have colored
their teeth with blueberry juice
and are giggling in the hammock.
The hammock is suspended between
a plum and apple tree, and when our wild,
whooping kids shake fruit from the trees,
we all dash for them to see if they are ready
to devour, one after the next,
pulling the sun into our bodies.

MR. TEZOZOMOC

Cuamochtlis[1]

Grandma would not let us play by the river anymore. She said it had not rained much this year and if we went into the water it would make us sick. She said we were already tired and that would only make things worse. We asked her if we could play with the kids down the way and she told us the other families had begun to move away to other towns, cities, and valleys.

We were sad because Rosa and Jose were moving away and we were not. She said it was because the communal granaries were empty, and they could not take any more years of drought; bad corn harvest, weak beans, the pestilence of the decaying carcasses of cows, horses, goats, sheep, chickens, and even household cats.

Grandpa, dad, and mom had gone ahead, to find a place for us to live. They were still strong, not my like grandma and us; Pedro, Juan, Maria, and me. We were too weak and hungry to make the long journey.

Grandma was sad and tired and she encouraged us by saying, "Eat the huamuchilles."

It was all we had to eat. We ate huamuchilles. We were hungry to the bone.

During the night Pedro had passed out near the arroyo. In the morning we just could not wake him up. We dragged him away from the dried river bed. Pedro's hands had not been able to dig deep enough to get water.

He was thirsty. He was hungry.

We had heard his echoes all night, but we could barely move. "Me estoy muriendo de hambre." "Me estoy muriendo de hambre." "Me estoy muriendo de hambre." "I am dying of hunger." I tossed but his words still nipped my cold earlobes. Grandma had attempted getting up, but she too was tired and went back to bed. Maria was scared and I could hear her murmur against Grandma. In the morning Grandma called to him many times but he would not come.

None of us could move much. Stomach bloated with painful gas. We looked at each other. As if to convince that beyond the pain, hunger gnawed the hairs on our necks.

Grandma would not let us help her bury Pedro. She said it would tire us out. Instead she sent us for firewood, warning not to tire over big logs, but to look for dried small branches. She said looking away, "We are having soup tonight."

By late afternoon we had collected about two feet of dried branches, and grandma had not returned.

We helped Maria get water from an almost dried pool. We stopped in front of the porch tired. Tired we were. We rested because we were tired and hungry. We helped Maria get the water filled cántaro off her shoulder.

Grandma was back and had started the fire. She was happy we were back. We rested because we were tired and hungry. We were unwilling to admit to each other the extent of our acheful hunger.

Grandma woke us up from our dreams of food. She leads us to the table where the bowls of steamy soup were waiting with ringlets of grease floating on the surface.

Our mouths melting with an outrush of saliva, ready to digest. We ate, and ate, and ate till we were heavy to our groins.

I laid there, on the floor, on those stretched out burlap sacks and the woolen blanket I shared with Juan. I could not go to sleep because the soup kept swooshing inside me and I could not get Pedro out of me.

I kept wondering where grandma had gotten the chicken.

I wish I would have eaten huamuchilles instead.

---

[1]Cuahmochtlis are an edible black seeded-fruit with green bitter husk. Pithecellobium dulce.

ROSS THOMPSON

Returns
for Dad

A golden bottle, cool and smooth as a singing stone,
rests in my infant palm, wet with condensation
straight from the fridge. I know the ridges and trade name
as I have downed enough flutes of Brown Lemonade
to launch a thousand ships. A kindly uncle sneaks
them from the bottling plant at the end of each week:
Cream Soda, Red Kola and Orange Crush.
I love it when, uncapped, chilled fizz can rush
into the mouth: a bolt of cold nectar,
a slug of brambly Sarsaparilla
that hits the back of the throat like a ghost
train run off the rails. The smooth syrup coats
my windpipe on the way down south, dances
on my tongue and the gap where my tonsils
once hung. We chug bottles dry and pretend
they are full of beer, tilted up on end
to be kissed mouth to mouth like an angel's
trumpet. I am lightheaded and grateful,
less so for the noxious cigarettes
my uncle smokes, and therefore for the debt
he cannot repay. Once empty, we bring
back the bottles in bags of light that sing
a song of what they used to hold, returned
for chocolate money that we had not earned.

Previously published in Threading The Light (Dedalus Press, 2019).

Leaving Home

mom's been gone
over a year, now,
and dad's moving
to a retirement residence,
so my siblings and I
sort through
hand-sewn quilts,
plates and dishes
that bear the nicks and scars
of a thousand meals,
tins that once held cookies
or snacks for backyard picnics,
and all the while
I'm seeking a vessel large enough
to carry the memory
of the smell of fresh-cut
Christmas trees
and my mother's baking

KERRY TRAUTMAN

Late Night Supper

After a long long hot spring workday
with my husband, some
sweat-stressed hollering in the work truck,
I flipped on the backyard light,
stirred mushrooms,
red pepper hunks—
oiled on a slip of foil—
and Italian sausage links
on the grill.

The neighbors all had finished
making love, were now
brushing teeth, contemplating
whether to keep windows open overnight,
or shut them against maybe storms.

Heat lightning pulsed across
eastern cloudbanks.
I sniffed the air for new ozone, for
if I needed more garlic,
watched thunderless lightning—
woeful without its rumbles—
strained to hear spring peepers over
my sizzle,
to see dark flight shadows in
the blackblue clouded sky.

I wondered if I should go in
and tell my husband
supper was nearly done,
or let the scent through the window
tell him for me.

Previously published in Mock Turtle Zine, 2017.

ANASTASIA VASSOS

Truly, Really

This almost-October afternoon of Indian summer
is so filled with light, the sun so yellow
the air, like butter, melts in my mouth,
bakes apples on the tongue.

This bitter-ash season of your death,
when we lit yellow candles that burned long and bright,
little chevrons of pain painting to heaven,
the air close, the heart closed.

Rosy morning opened her robe in the rain, and shivered.
Now the day is so filled with sun, so filled with heat,
I could weep. I was eight when you brought us

fresh figs, your pleasure spilling like warm syrup,
the afternoon ablaze like this one. Eat, you said,
they ripened in the sun, you won't believe the taste.

ELINOR ANN WALKER

In Praise of Garlic

Allium sounds pleasant not odorous,
far smoother on the tongue than *garleac*,
names for things that flavor breath, broth, braises
(both words seem obscure if not archaic).
Tenacious peels stick, hold one hand hostage;
skins cling tight to my fingers as I chop.
Even cloves limned with green sprouts face carnage.
Oven-side, the dogs, hoping that I'll drop
anything but lines, doubt gods and monsters;
my knife knocks a verse; I hear spells and odes.
May this ordinary spear-leek augur
good—unnerve vampires, all shifting shapes—bode
well. Bits sizzle in the skillet. We wait,
the dogs and I, for magic on the plate.

LAURA GRACE WELDON

Yeast

I wait in single-celled quiescence till
you wake me with warm water and honey,
feed me grain, knead me under your hands
to a tuneless hum your grandmothers
sing through you.

The sound enters me.
So does your breath
and what your skin says.
So does a quiet knowing
offered by this counter, this room.

You anoint me with oil,
leave me to rest under cloth,
believe I will rise. I do, full and round.
Rise again in the pan, abundant, ready
to die so I might nourish you.

Previously published in Portals (Middle Creek, 2021).

KORY WELLS

Some Notes and Three Word Problems on Red Velvet Cake

Cousin, wasn't red velvet cake the glory
at those family Christmases? Like a red-robed chorister
it sang the call to worship from the altar of our bountiful desserts,
four layers of rich wonder, pure white boiled frosting,
a sprinkling of coconut and pecans. I find the recipe
years later in Grandmother's tattered three-ring binder.
It calls for an entire two-ounce bottle of red food coloring,
a half cup of Crisco, and a teaspoon of butter flavoring. If desired.

∞

The black nurse expertly thumps the pale crook of my arm.
I have to look away before the stick.
You've got pretty blood, she says. I'm reassured.
And skeptical. Everyone's blood isn't pretty?
Oh no. I wonder, that this could be true.

It is true that in the 1870s, the Juneteenth drink of choice
was lemonade tinted red for the blood shed by slaves.

∞

Word problem: If in the white woman's veins
there are one hundred drops of blood,
one and a half of which are from Sub-Saharan Africa,
does that knowledge change her?
Answer in complete sentences, accounting for
the likes of Dr. Walter Plecker,
who lobbied the one-drop rule into Virginia law:
any child with a single drop of black blood
categorized as black. Natives forced
to register as black. Explain why
this has been called bureaucratic genocide.

∞

It may be true that Betty and John Adams of Texas
on a trip to New York City ate the most divine
red velvet cake at the Waldorf. It is true they gave away,
at grocers, full-color recipe cards pretty enough to eat.
Their recipe, of course, called for Adams Extract
food coloring. And vanilla. And butter flavoring.

∞

Some people claim red food coloring has no flavor.
I don't believe this is true. It is true that
in 1894 the Supreme Court in Plumley vs. Massachusetts
said that food coloring serves only to delude customers.

∞

Word problem: Two cousins who've never met
walk into a cupcake shop lined with glass cases
of curvaceously topped confections, every imaginable flavor.
Calculate the likelihood both cousins will choose
red velvet. For extra credit, using genetic markers,
calculate their expected differential in skin tone.

∞

It is true I was a grown woman with children
before I realized red velvet cake is made with cocoa.

∞

My mother says the family sometimes wondered
if they had a little black blood. There was that cousin
with the nappy hair. Mostly they talked about being Cherokee.

Did you know brown sugar used to be called red sugar?

∞

Butter flavoring became popular when butter
was rationed in World War II. Thirty years later,
Grandmother was still using it in recipes.

∞

When two people, one black, one white,
discover they're a DNA match
and find each other on Facebook,
name the force that keeps them from posting
for all the world to see: *This is my cousin.*

∞

Walter Plecker is remembered as a rigid man who never
smiled. In his black and white world, how could he
ever have enjoyed a slice of Grandmother's red velvet cake?

∞

Cousin, I hope you'll come for red velvet cake.
I'll bake an all-natural version with beet juice and butter.
We'll trace our fingers on the family tree
to the grandmother we share—
Mahaley or Lucretia or one of the unnamed—
and imagine her singing from heaven to all
her children, hallelujah. With your slice of cake,
I'll offer you the gooey crumbs and frosting
that cling to the knife after the cut—messy
but my favorite part.

∞

Word problem: If you dispense two fluid ounces of red food coloring
drop by drop, how many drops will you count?
And how long will this take?

MARCELINE WHITE

Personal Etymology of Mush

Believing in Manifest Destiny, mush goes on a journey, advances from France across the Atlantic, finds itself fixed up with fry bread in First Nation fires. A farmhouse favorite, mush gets around: from Cole Camp, Missouri, kitchens to Midwest menus, a brunch favorite and diner staple. Among the Romany, mush is a friend; with the Brits, a mouth, a face. Mush can be cloying or overly sentimental, it's true, but look— an old man's face. Caterpillar eyebrows heap over sky-blue eyes. He shakes his scratched black skillet as butter sizzles the mass of masa in the pan. Coffee brews beside him, as he pierces the pieces with tin fork tines, held in his crooked right hand. He softly croons off-key his favorite Irish folk song, puts sunshine on our waiting plates.

Mush: All my love poems are about my grandfather.

JINN BUG & RON WHITEHEAD

Soup Town Days

The blue and white graffiti on the alley wall reads
Kes kannatab, see kaua elab. "Do you have English?"
the old man asks a passerby. "Can you tell me what
this means?" The young woman he's stopped says,
"Of course! It is 'Who suffers the most, lives the longest,'"
and this is why the old man is thinking about suffering
as he follows the sound of singing down the steep hill
to the festival by the edge of the Emajõgi.

He has seen a poster pasted to a door and after puzzled
head-scratching deciphers Supilinn as "Soup Town."
He imagines he will find a crowd gathered around long
tables of deliciousness as Estonian mothers and grand-
mothers vie for medals—who has the best meat soup,
milk soup with pearl barley, herring stew, cabbage cream?
Won't he try this bread soup with its incense of apple and
cinnamon tickling his nose? The old man is ravenous;

he has been hungry for days now. Every backyard in Estonia
has a dozen fruit trees bursting into flower, long rows of carefully
pruned and trained raspberry canes, black currant bushes,
sandy earth tilled and frilled with strawberries, carrots, beets,
rhubarb, turnips and also tiny greenhouses with grapevines
snaking through the panes. As he hobbles down to Soup Town,
he admires an old, gnarled plum, tortured yet still flowering—
Just as I am, he thinks—surely this passion for growing food

is a remnant of the years of occupation. He imagines how
it was to queue through the long hours of the night, hoping
morning would bring bread, a packet of sugar, cooking oil
while the Soviets broke bountiful family farms apart, forced
collectivized farmers to grow according to plans drafted by
the uncalloused hands of bureaucrats and to sell at fixed prices.
Who is he to grumble in a land of plenty where thousands
died from malnutrition and the wisdom of the State?

There is something noble in suffering, something sacred.
He thinks of his own childhood in the farmlands of Kentucky,
how his mother would send him to pull corn or cucumbers
from fields of river-sweetened soil, how he'd creep down to
the cellar to retrieve a jar of pickles or beans from long shelves
ranged against starvation wages. His family knew how to
make do, carry on without complaint, and there was always
a little extra to help someone who suffered more than
they suffered. A good attitude and a bowl of soup shared?

Why, there was a double helping of salvation to beat back any
bad time. He remembers huddling in the cold dark attic over
the kitchen, wind whistling through the walls, listening to his
father tell a joke he'd heard at the coal mines to his mother,
her laughter bubbling up from below as she fried eggs for their
breakfast and the ragged rooster crowed the coming dawn.
To this day, he blesses his parents for showing him how
hard work and unrelenting humor feed endurance; nothing
can break him if he holds fast to joy. When he reaches the park
overlooking the Emajõgi, there is no soup.

People have spread blankets and sheets covered with used
books and toys, worn jeans, all for sale. He asks the man selling
ancient postcards, "Where is the soup?" and the man says, "Ah,
Soup Town is what we call this place. Poor people lived here
and had many gardens and each street is a food: Melon, Berry,
Pea, Potato. Mix streets together, make a good soup!"

He laughs and the old man laughs too. He sees the boy,
standing on a large wooden swing with ten others, sailing up
and down above a chattering, laughing crowd.
"You try külakiik?" the man says. "Every village has this swing.
It is important to swing together, have fun, yes?" Children
dressed as superheroes twirl folk dances before a stage
where fifty men and women sing in clear high harmony and the
audience sings along. Everyone must know all the words to
every song. A girl races past him, waving a torch which she

plunges into a huge pile of dry evergreen brush and the dusk
comes alive with towering fire. Showering sparks singe the old
man's face and he steps back into the shelter of the crowd.
He thinks of Buddha teaching that a man shot by pain's arrow
who responds with grief and laments, who beats his breast

in distress, shoots himself with a second arrow, this one
deep-piercing his mind; how a wise man understands it is only
the body suffering and refuses to let pain shatter his soul.
The old man has forgotten his hunger. His heart is humming,

drunk as bees in pollen time. It's time to swing,
it's time to sing, it is time to laugh in Soup Town
where there is no soup yet the twisted trees in flower,
each chorus sounding in the night, the fire itself breathes
Endure, Endure, Endure and you will triumph.

SCOTT WIGGERMAN

Midwest Corn Roast

Old cinder blocks held up
a row of four twin bedsprings,
high enough that a rake
could distribute the hot coals
under each three- by six-foot space.

On the springs were dozens
of ears of corn, soaked in trash cans
of water overnight, silks removed,
husks tightly rewrapped.
Local farmers and veterans
monitored the roasting corn,
adding, turning, removing them
with long-handled shovels
in between sips of Schlitz.

Corn fields and stands abounded,
a baker's dozen for a dollar,
so corn was served at supper
all summer long—but boiled,
served with bright yellow pronged
holders shaped like mini-cobs.

Roasting was special,
stripped back husks provided
a means to grip, revealing
slightly browned, sometimes charred
niblets at their sweetest—no need
for butter or salt, though most folks
added plenty of both.

Boys would dare each other
to see who could eat the most ears.
Some ate "typewriter style," the length

of a row and back; some ate
"beaver style," round and round the cob,
teeth gnashing a third at a time.
The unspoken rule? No leaving
any niblet on the cob, not even
the baby ones near the silk end.

Most boys had not yet heard
of Vietnam, though some would
soon come back in boxes from there.
Other boys would move
as far from Illinois as they could,
but most would stay, and some
would become the men roasting corn
over bedsprings for a new generation,
not a one as innocent as these.

AMELIA L. WILLIAMS

My Brother's Gift of the Palobar Cookbook

"In this house, we're all mongrels....united by our passion for food..."

Start a few weeks early. Order Mediterranean
mixes from the Spice Diva. Send your eldest
for lemons. Organic, but alas, not unwaxed.
The internet provideth—how to pour boiling
water to slip off paraffin film. Twelve lemons,
three canning jars, a lot of olive oil and salt.
Wait two weeks. Now brown cumin seeds
in a dry pan—aroma rises, like leather-scented
tobacco mixed with anise.

      Pulse cured lemons
to a delicate orange-tinged paste with cumin
and sweet paprika. Leftover lemony oil is a bonus.
To prepare tzatziki, first make labneh. Drip
whey from a mix of Greek and whole
milk yogurts in your old gold coffee filter,
well-washed. This is where za'atar comes in
with its peppery grass scent. Out into April's frosty
garden I go to find early sprouts of mint nosing
up near last year's dried stems.

      Fresh is best. Sumac
pounded to burgundy powder is for oil-tossed red
onions sliced thin as ghosts, also coriander-jazzed
after toasting and grinding by hand in mom's mortar.
Lovingly rub lamb shoulder with harissa and cured
lemon paste. Let sit overnight.

      Roast at hottest setting
fifteen minutes per side, sunchokes and carrots
coarsely chopped into the roasting pan. Pour boiling
water over and braise with vegetables low and slow for
six to seven hours. Now you're free to mash jalapenos
and cilantro into a paste called schug,

                              and lightly grill
pita with olive oil, arrange hand-painted Kütahya
carnation- and tulip-patterned condiment bowls
on the outside table in the order of assembly.
Then froth up coriander-infused crème anglaise
for tahini ice cream you made last night.

                         Caramelize
pears in butter to serve on the side. With a waffle cookie.
Pulled lamb on grilled buns. Next year maybe I'll try
the traditional bread—Yemeni kubaneh—plan ahead.

SUSAN WOLBARST

Chanterelles

(For Frank and Kathy)

Slightly ruffled parasols,
their golden glowing
hides demurely
under dry pine needles.
The older ones turn orange.
Sliced thin, sautéed in olive oil,
their texture barely stiffens.
With shredded parmesan,
topping a cracker-thin pizza,
they taste of earth's
rich secrets, of discovery,
of erotic dreams,
of life's fragile luck.

CHRISTOPHER WOODS

Hunger

Reading it for the third time, I am still amazed. Hungry, after midnight, in a hotel room in Galveston, I scan the room service menu in my lap. There, under the "Omelets" heading, it states that all are served with warm biscuits and yes, with mourning potatoes.

I am astounded. But I am also a realist and do not believe that biscuits will climb five floors and arrive still warm at my door. That they arrive at all is sufficient. Still, it distresses me to know that I have, for all this time, through all kinds of culinary weather, never known that some potatoes, by design or scheme or recipe, are meant only for mourning. I have eaten potatoes in all kinds of moods, even outside my homeland, and never once, I think, funereally.

But I am also starving. I pick up the phone and call room service, order the potatoes without question, in an almost normal voice. Then, waiting in the dark, I hear waves crashing against the seawall. The world is such an eerie place, I think, each day stranger than the one before.

Somewhere in the bowels of this hotel a room service cart is rolling this way, and for an instant I do not care if even death comes riding on it.

ROBERT WYNNE

Creation Myth: Toast

The stubborn sun rose, not at the urgent request
of any god, but because it couldn't sleep any longer.
Bread brushed crumbs from its face and remembered

last night's dream, the crunching sounds like footsteps
on fresh snow. The knife, when it came, was a relief
from the simple sentence imposed on each loaf

by oven after oven, with their promises and lies.
Crust crumbled at the edges, and questioned
how dawn light stretched the blade's shadow

past the table and onto the floor. It is important
to remember that fire is a form of love, the way
energy embraces some things until they become

something entirely new. So it was that flames
tongued the soft slice until it blushed golden brown.
So it was that even peanut butter softened

at the sight of such beauty, and grain learned
what it could be: crisp and hot, firmer over time
and able to carry so much on its back. Still,

no one knows what hand guided the transformation
but toast has no time for such mundane concerns.

SARAH YASIN

I Serve it Forth

Come. Sit on my lap.

I shall feed you whole

pleasures from my hand:

blueberry waffles with

smooth clotted cream,

strong Irish coffee,

currants and cherries,

pastry with mascarpone.

I shall place fine delectation

into your mouth and you

will stretch up for more.

HIROMI YOSHIDA

Grandmother's Kitchen

That dark unlit space,
a haven for my grandmother,
shuffling, groping
around for some odd,
forgotten thing—nothing
as handy, or American,
as Tupperware, nor
as concrete as that one
missing chopstick, but
necessary, nonetheless. Yet,

she'd managed
to pickle *oshinko* cucumbers
and eggplants, the *nuka-miso* stench
being her friend—to emerge from that dark,
unlikely space with a plate of ground beef omelet—
a miracle, considering her aversion to butter—
"*Bata-kusai*," she'd mutter
about anything "Western" (I suppose my
white *gaijin* boyfriends reeked
of butter, too, like overfed geese). That

kitchen had been
her inviolate space that Banana
Yoshimoto would've praised to the white-
tiled skies (had it been visible)—*nuka-miso* reek
and incense fragrance intermingling in a pungent
vapory dance throughout that ramshackle two-
storied house in *Suna-machi* till my

mother modernized Grandmother's kitchen: she
flooded electric lights into it—plastered mildewed
      wood walls with pink rose vinyl wallpaper—crammed the latest
refrigerator model with
      meat and dairy products [blocks of *Yuki-Jirushi* butter] for me
and Mei-Mei, who'd
      grown into a long-legged American teenager in the porous City
of Sand.

Since that kitchen makeover,
Grandmother would appear before us (while
we watched Madonna writhing
like a fallen snake goddess on MTV), kimono-less, muttering to herself,
her flattened-out, shriveled-up breasts exposed—
a grey specter we ignored. But, Mother
said *Obaa-chan* loved the new microwave
that steamed leftover rice to perfect white fluff.

Previously published in Gidra, No. 6 (June 2021), and in Epicanthus (Finishing Line Press, 2021).

Afterword

Without food we are nothing. That and sleep, but sleeping is interesting only for the dreams. Food, on the other hand, delights and torments, and, we must have it. Several times a day, if possible.

I met Brennan Breeland in an online food writing class. Before that it had never occurred to me that the love of food and the love of words could be such a powerful recipe. In the class forum, Brennan and I started talking about the possibilities, which led, after several years, to this book.

It wasn't as easy as either of us expected and we spent far longer than the profession generally takes. If not for Emily Liner's repeated reinvigoration from the publisher's end, this project would have been just so many pixels decaying in the ether.

But, hunger wins out.

Whether sweet or sour, nutritious or guilty pleasure, these poems chart the human intersection with the foods we eat, the beverages we drink. And, it's not just the eating. Foods come with associations, sometimes called baggage. The brain links foods we eat with people we love – or hate – and nothing we can do will separate those connections. Comfort foods are not eaten for the calories but for the emotions they hold, sustenance of a different kind. And these poems may ping those undefined emotional taste buds, and you remember events from people long gone or trials recently overcome.

Thanks for taking time to savor the poems here. Just like the foods, the poets themselves are varied, each seasoned from a heritage that differs from all others. Most are from the United States, but like all good recipes, flavors from farther afield bring the final dish to completion.

Maybe eating and sleeping are not so different after all. The places these poems go will fill your harvest basket with dreams, real memories as well as never-ventured cupboards. And who can resist the urge to eat?

Bon appetit!

Stan Galloway
Mathias, WV

About the Editors

BRENNAN BREELAND is an eater, drinker, lawyer, veteran, writer, and raconteur from Brookhaven, Mississippi. He has moved to New York City to taste life in Technicolor with his brilliant wife and two spoiled dogs: one a tyrannical malcontent, the other a well-meaning doofus. He loves boiled peanuts, raw oysters, chop-cheese sandwiches, fried chicken, shrimp Creole, dumplings of all kinds, and wine from the Southern Rhône and Champagne in equal measure.

STAN GALLOWAY writes from the hills of West Virginia. He has written and edited several collections of poetry, including *Endlessly Rocking* (Unbound Content, 2019), a celebration of Walt Whitman's 200th birthday. He hosted a panel discussion on Food and Poetry at Pier-Glass Poetry. In addition to poetry, seafood and sweets are his weaknesses.

Contributors

SANDRA ANFANG is a poet, teacher, and artist who lives in the California wine country north of San Francisco. She's worked as a librarian, archaeological field hand, picture framer, teacher, puppeteer, clown, silversmith, tutor, and at jobs whose titles she can't remember. She teaches poetry writing to kids from elementary through high school. Her poetry collections include *Looking Glass Heart* (Finishing Line Press, 2016), *Road Worrier: Poems of the Inner and Outer Landscape* (Finishing Line Press, 2018), and *Xylem Highway* (Main Street Rag, 2019). To write, for her, is to breathe. Visit her at sandeanfangart.com

BARTHOLOMEW BARKER is one of the organizers of Living Poetry, a collection of poets and poetry lovers in the Triangle region of North Carolina. His first poetry collection, *Wednesday Night Regular*, written in and about strip clubs, was published in 2013. His second, *Milkshakes and Chilidogs*, a chapbook of food inspired poetry was served in 2017. Born and raised in Ohio, studied in Chicago, he worked in Connecticut for nearly twenty years before moving to Hillsborough where he makes money as a computer programmer to fund his poetry habit. bartbarkerpoet.com

DAISY BASSEN is a poet and practicing physician who graduated from Princeton University's Creative Writing Program and completed her medical training at The University of Rochester and Brown. Her work has appeared in *Oberon*, *McSweeney's* and *[PANK]* among other journals. She was the winner of the 2019 So to Speak Poetry Contest, the 2019 ILDS White Mice Contest and the 2020 Beullah Rose Poetry Prize. Born and raised in New York, she now lives in Rhode Island with her family.

CHARLIE BECKER is a speech and language pathologist who also studies and writes poetry with the Community Literature Initiative (CLI) in Los Angeles. His poems tend to be about art, nature, food, and relationships (sometimes all in the same poem). Some of Charlie's poems have been published in *The Comstock Review*, *Passager*, *Oyster River Review*, *Silver Pinion*, and *Months to Years*. He lives in Laguna Woods, California.

CLAIRE BOOKER lives in Brighton, UK. Her latest poetry collection is *A Pocketful of Chalk* (Arachne Press) and her pamphlets are *The Bone That Sang* (Indigo Dreams) and *Later There Will Be Postcards* (Green Bottle Press). She has worked as a journalist and herbalist, and enjoys concocting her own wines, jams and poems. Her works has appeared widely, including in *Agenda, Magma, The Rialto, The Spectator* and in *Moving Images* edited by Jennifer Maloney and Bart White. More info at bookerplays.co.uk

DESPY BOUTRIS's writing has been published or is forthcoming in *Copper Nickel, Ploughshares, Crazyhorse, AGNI, American Poetry Review, The Gettysburg Review, Colorado Review*, and elsewhere. Currently, she serves as Editor-in-Chief of The West Review.

After being homeless in her teens, CATHY BRYANT worked as a life model, shoe shop assistant, civil servant, and childminder before writing professionally. She has won 29 literary awards, including the Bulwer-Lytton Fiction Prize and the Wergle Flomp Award, and her work has been published all over the world. She co-edited the anthologies *Best of Manchester Poets 1, 2 and 3*, and Cathy's own collections are *Contains Strong Language and Scenes of a Sexual Nature, Look at All the Women* and *Erratics*. Cathy lives in Manchester, UK. See Cathy's listings for impoverished writers at compsandcalls.com/wp

BETT BUTLER's poetry and short fiction have appeared in *Weave, Feathertale, Amp*, and other small-press publications in the U.S. and Canada. An award-winning songwriter and jazz musician (International Songwriting Competition, Independent Music Awards), she co-owns Mandala Music Production in San Antonio, Texas, where she and her spouse produce music and spoken word licensed for HBO, Discovery Channel, and more.

JINN BUG is a poet, photographer, gardener, activist, visual artist and life-long dreamer. Her photography, vignettes, and poems have appeared in *Appalachian Heritage, New Southerner, LEO Weekly, Fiolet & Wing—An Anthology of Domestic Fabulism, Aquillrelle, For Sale, Pure Uncut Candy, The Rooted Reader, Gyroscope Review, Necro Magazine* and other print and online publications. Her most recent book of poetry is *Nights at the Museum*. Visit her at JinnBug.com.

KIRSTEN CASEY is a California Poet in the Schools, and has one collection of poetry, *Ex Vivo: Out of the Living Body*, published by Hip Pocket Press. She is in her third year as Poet Laureate of Nevada County, California, and her second collection of poems, *Grieving Birds*, was a recent finalist for the Gunpowder Press Dryden-Vreeland book prize.

GABRIEL CLEVELAND is a poet and fiction writer with an MFA from the Solstice Creative Writing Program. Along with press founder Joan Cusack Handler, he co-edited *Places We Return To*, a 20th Anniversary retrospective on the publishing history of CavanKerry Press, where he serves as Managing Editor and Director. An avid video gamer and music lover, he hosts The Andover Special, a weekly internet radio program on HomeGrownRadioNJ.com. Gabriel is also a mental health advocate, often working online to raise awareness, visibility, and money for psychological and psychosocial issues. He has spent several years in the field of caregiving for people with increased physical and/or mental needs and wants you to know that you're not alone.

TERENCE CULLETON has published several collections of formally crafted narrative and lyric poems, including *A Communion of Saints* (2011) and *Eternal Life* (2015), both with Anaphora Literary Press. His most recent book of sonnets, *A Tree and Gone*, is through Future Cycle Press. Mr. Culleton has published in numerous journals and reviews and his work has been featured on NPR. He reads widely throughout the Philadelphia and New York areas. terenceculletonpoetry.com

STEVE CUSHMAN is the author of three novels, including *Portisville*, winner of the 2004 Novello Literary Award. He has published two poetry chapbooks, and his first full-length collection, *How Birds Fly*, won the 2018 Lena Shull Book award. His latest collection, *The Last Time*, was published by Unicorn Press in 2023. Cushman lives in Greensboro, North Carolina, and works in the IT department at Cone Health.

JOHN DAVIS is the author of *Gigs* and *The Reservist*. His work has appeared recently in *DMQ Review, Iron Horse Literary Review* and *Terrain.org*. He lives on an island in the Salish Sea.

JOHN DORROH prefers riding his bike on dedicated trails beside corn fields and over rusted bridges over work-outs with Peloton. He likes to find new eateries and pubs along the way. He appreciates the power of home-baked bread, real butter, red wine, and bourbon. He once baked treats with monks in Austria and consumed a healthy portion of their beer. Five of his poems were nominated for Best of the Net. Others have appeared in *Feral, River Heron, Kissing Dynamite*, and *Big Windows Review*. He had two chapbooks published in 2022 and is waiting for word on his third.

JENNIFER R. EDWARDS is a speech-language pathologist from Vermont and currently residing in Concord, NH. Her Pushcart Prize (XLIV) nominated poetry appears online and in *Portrait of New England*, *The Ekphrastic Review*, *Headline Poetry and Press*, *Lucky Jefferson*, *FreezeRay Poetry*, *4linesart.com*, *COVID Spring: Granite State Pandemic Poems* (Hobblebush Books, 2020) and was honorably mentioned for the 2020 NEPC Amy Lowell Prize (selected by Dzvinia Orlowsky). She was a 2021 Thomas Lux Poetry Fellow at Palm Beach Poetry Festival. She currently curates for *Button Poetry*. Twitter @Jennife00420145 Instagram JenEdwards8

LINDA MCCAULEY FREEMAN is the author of the forthcoming full-length poetry collection *The Marriage Manual* (Backroom Window Press, 2024) and *The Family Plot: Poems* (Backroom Window Press, 2022) and has been widely published in international journals, including in a Chinese translation. She was nominated for a Pushcart Prize and has been the featured U.S. poet in *The Poet Magazine* and won Grand Prize in StoriArts' Maya Angelou poetry contest. Lines from her poem Made in America were selected by Kwame Alexander to use in his Civil Community Poem and are on display at the Civil Rights Memorial Museum in Montgomery, Alabama. She has an MFA from Bennington College and is the former poet-in-residence of the Putnam Arts Council. She lives in the Hudson Valley, NY, where she is a swing dance teacher and a yoga instructor. Follow her at LindaMcCauleyFreeman.com, Facebook: LindaMcCauleyFreeman and Twitter: LindaMccFreeman

KATHERINE GAFFNEY completed her MFA at the University of Illinois at Urbana-Champaign and is currently working on her PhD at the University of Southern Mississippi. Her work has previously appeared or is forthcoming in *jubilat*, *Rabbit Catastrophe*, *Harpur Palate*, *the Mississippi Review*, *Meridian*, *the Tampa Review*, and elsewhere. Her first chapbook, *Once Read as Ruin*, is forthcoming from Finishing Line Press.

Writer, teacher, and rabbinic deputy, REUVEN GOLDFARB has published poetry, stories, essays, articles, and Torah commentary in scores of periodicals and anthologies and won several awards. He co-founded and edited *Agada*, the illustrated Jewish literary magazine, and taught English at Oakland's Merritt College. He now serves as copy editor for books and manuscripts and coordinates monthly meetings for the Upper Galilee branch of Voices Israel. Residents of Tzfat since 2001, he and his wife Yehudit founded Bayt Maor HaLev Center for Movement, Healing, and Language Arts. They host classes and a weekly Talmud study session in their home. Visit soundcloud.com/reuven-goldfarb and YouTube.

ERICA GOSS lives in Eugene, Oregon, where she teaches, writes and edits the newsletter *Sticks & Stones*. Recent and upcoming publications include *Creative Nonfiction, North Dakota Quarterly, Spillway, A-Minor, Redactions, Consequence, Slant, The Sunlight Press, The Pedestal, San Pedro River Review*, and *Critical Read*.

CONNIE JORDAN GREEN lives on a farm in East Tennessee where she writes and gardens. She is the author of two award-winning novels for young people, *The War at Home* and *Emmy*, published originally by Margaret McElderry imprint of MacMillan and Simon Shuster, respectively, reissued in soft cover by Tellico Books imprint of Iris Press; two poetry chapbooks, *Slow Children Playing* and *Regret Comes to Tea*; and two poetry collections, *Household Inventory*, 2015, winner of the Brick Road Poetry Award, and *Darwin's Breath* (Iris Press). She frequently leads writing workshops.

GEORGE GUIDA is author of nine books, including the novel *Posts from Suburbia* (Encircle Publications, 2022) and five collections of poems, most recently *Zen of Pop* (Long Sky Media, 2020) and *New York and Other Lovers* (Encircle Publications, 2020).

MRINALINI HARCHANDRAI is from Mumbai, India. Her first novel, *Rescuing a River Breeze* (Bloomsbury India, 2023), was longlisted for the McKitterick Prize 2021. Her short stories have been longlisted for the Commonwealth Short Story Prize 2018 and selected as a Top Pick (2018) with Juggernaut Books, India. Her work has been anthologized in The *Brave New World of Goan Writing 2018-19* and *RLFPA Editions' Best Indian Poetry 2018*.

J. DAVID HARPER wrote those movies you never saw and those books you didn't read. He has published short fiction, essays, and poetry in places such as *Flash Fiction Magazine, Right Hand Pointing, Front Porch Review, Altered Reality Magazine, Potato Soup Journal*, and *The Haven*. He can be found online at thedavidharper.com.

MUREALL HEBERT lives near Seattle, WA. Her work can be found in *trampset, Tab Journal, Arc Poetry Magazine, Qu, The Normal School, The Adirondack Review, Carve, Hobart, [PANK], decomP*, and elsewhere. She's been nominated for Best Microfiction, Best New Poets, and a Pushcart Prize. Mureall holds an MFA from the Northwest Institute of Literary Arts. You can find her online @mureallhebert andmureallhebert.com

EMILY HOCKADAY is the author of *In a Body* (Harbor Editions 2023), *Naming the Ghost* (Cornerstone Press 2022), and six chapbooks. She is a De Groot Foundation Writer of Note and a Café Royal Cultural Foundation, NY City Artist Corps, and NYFA Queens Art Fund recipient. Her poems have appeared in numerous literary journals in print and online, including *Electric Literature* and the *North American Review*. She is the editor of *Heartbeat of the Universe* (Interstellar Flight Press 2024). Emily writes about ecology, parenthood, the urban environment, and chronic illness. She can be found online at emilyhockaday.com and @E_Hockaday.

KAREN PAUL HOLMES won the 2023 Lascaux Poetry Prize and received a Special Mention in The Pushcart Prize Anthology. She has two books: *No Such Thing as Distance* (Terrapin) and *Untying the Knot* (Aldrich). Poetry credits include *The Writer's Almanac*, *The Slowdown*, *Verse Daily*, *Diode*, and *Plume*. She's also a freelance writer who teaches writing at various venues and conferences.

JOHN HOPPENTHALER's books of poetry are *Night Wing Over Metropolitan Area*, *Domestic Garden*, *Anticipate the Coming Reservoir*, and *Lives of Water*, all with Carnegie Mellon UP. With Kazim, Ali, he has co-edited a volume of essays on the poetry of Jean Valentine, *This-World Company* (U of Michigan Press). Professor of English at East Carolina University, his poetry, essays, and interviews have appeared in *Ploughshares*, *Virginia Quarterly Review*, *New York Magazine*, *Southern Review*, *Poetry Northwest*, *Blackbird*, *Southern Humanities Review*, and many other journals, anthologies, and textbooks.

Twice published in The New York Times, MARY LOUISE KIERNAN is the recipient of Tempe Public Library / Arizona State University's 2015 Poetry Prize and Queensborough Community College's Walt Whitman Excellence in Creative Writing Award. Her debut full-length collection from Kelsay Books is titled *The Gift of Glossophobia*. You are invited to visit her website at marylouisekiernan.com and to follow her on Instagram @postsbymarylouise.

EMILEE KINNEY hails from the small farm-town of Kenockee, Michigan, near one of the Great Lakes: Lake Huron. She received her MFA in poetry at SIU Carbondale and is currently pursuing her PhD at the University of Southern Mississippi. Her work has been published in *Passages North*, *West Trestle Review*, *Cider Press Review*, *SWWIM* and elsewhere. emileekinneypoetry.com

PHYLLIS KLEIN is a psychotherapist and poet from the San Francisco Bay Area. Her work has appeared in numerous journals and anthologies including *Chiron Review, Sweet, 3Elements, I-70*, the Minnesota Review, and *Gyroscope Review* among others. She was a finalist in the Sweet Poetry Contest, 2017, the Carolyn Forche Humanitarian Poetry Contest, 2019, and the Fischer Prize, 2019. She's been nominated for multiple Pushcart Prizes. Her new book, *The Full Moon Herald* from Grayson Books is a newspaper of poetry and has won honorable mention in poetry for the Eric Hoffer Book Award, 2021.

An artist, poet, and freelance writer, J.I. KLEINBERG lives in Bellingham, Washington, USA, and on Instagram @jikleinberg. Her chapbooks *The Word for Standing Alone in a Field* (Bottlecap Press), *how to pronounce the wind* (Paper View Books), and *Desire's Authority* (Ravenna Press Triple Series No. 23) were published in 2023; *she needs the river* was published by Poem Atlas in March 2024.

MIRIAM N. KOTZIN is the author of five collections of poetry, most recently, *Debris Field* (David Robert Books, 2017). Her collection of short fiction, *Country Music* (Spuyten Duyvil Press, 2017), joins a novel, The Real Deal (Brick House Press 2012), and a collection of flash fiction, *Just Desserts* (Star Cloud Press 2010). Her fiction and poetry have been published in anthologies and numerous periodicals such as *Shenandoah, Boulevard, SmokeLong Quarterly, Eclectica, Mezzo Cammin, Offcourse*, and *Valparaiso Poetry Review*. She teaches creative writing and literature at Drexel University.

MARK L. LEVINSON is a Hebrew-to-English translator, hailing from Greater Boston and living in Herzliya, Israel. His most recent translations include the novel *The Milk Moon Assassin*, by L.A. Couriel, and a book by Prof. Dina Porat about poet Abba Kovner and his plan for anti-Nazi vengeance.

RAYMOND LUCZAK is the author and editor of over 30 titles, including 12 full-length poetry collections such as *Chlorophyll* (Modern History Press), *Far from Atlantis* (Gallaudet University Press), and *Animals Out-There W-i-l-d* (Unbound Edition Press). His work has appeared in *POETRY, Prairie Schooner*, and elsewhere. An inaugural Zoeglossia Poetry Fellow, he lives in Minneapolis, Minnesota.

LINDA MALNACK is the author of two poetry chapbooks, *21 Boxes* (dancing girl press) and *Bone Beads* (Paper Boat Press). Her poetry appears in *Prairie Schooner, the Seattle Review, Amherst Review, Southern Humanities Review, Blackbird,* and elsewhere. Linda is an Assistant Poetry Editor for *Crab Creek Review.*

JOHN C. MANNONE has poems in *Windhover, North Dakota Quarterly, Poetry South, New England Journal Medicine,* and others. He was awarded a Jean Ritchie Fellowship (2017) in Appalachian literature and served as celebrity judge for the National Federation of State Poetry Societies (2018). A physicist, John lives in Knoxville, Tennessee.

KAREN GREENBAUM-MAYA is a retired clinical psychologist, former German major, and, two-time Pushcart and Best of the Net nominee, who learned to cook in self-defense. Besides her professional activities, she reviewed restaurants for the Claremont Courier for five years, sometimes in heroic couplets, sometimes imitating Hemingway. She has developed cookie recipes for industrial use. She co-curates Fourth Sundays, a long-running poetry series in Claremont, California.

MICHAEL MINGO is a poet and medical editor from Pittsburgh, Pennsylvania. He earned his MFA in poetry from the Johns Hopkins Writing Seminars, and his work has appeared in Spillway, RHINO, Third Coast, and The McNeese Review, among other journals.

THOMAS MIXON has poems and stories in Rattle, Variant Literature, Epiphany Magazine, and elsewhere. He's a Pushcart and Best of the Net nominee. He's trying to write a few books.

WILDA MORRIS's first book of poetry, Szechwan Shrimp & Fortune Cookies: Poems from a Chinese Restaurant, was published in 2008. Her most recent book, Pequod Poems: Gamming with Moby-Dick was published in 2009. Wilda is the workshop chairperson for Poets & Patrons of Chicago and a former president of the Illinois State Poetry Society. She is widely published, and has won awards for free and formal verse and haiku. Her blog, at wildamorris.blogspot.com, provides a monthly contest for other poets.

JILL MUNRO has been published in major poetry magazines including *The Frogmore Press, Popshot Quarterly, The Fenland Reed* and *The Rialto* and her work has also been anthologised by The Emma Press, Candlestick Press, Paper Swans Press & Calder Valley Press. She won the O'Bheal Five Words International Poetry competition 2017/18 and was 2nd placed in this year's competition. Jill's first collection *Man from La Paz* was published in 2015 by Green Bottle Press. She won the Fair Acre Press

Pamphlet Competition 2015 with *The Quilted Multiverse*, published April 2016 and has been long-listed on several occasions for the National Poetry Competition. Jill was awarded a Hawthornden Fellowship for 2018. She lives and writes in the depths of Ashdown Forest, Sussex, England.

SHARON LASK MUNSON is a retired teacher, poet, old movie enthusiast, lover of road trips, with many published poems, two chapbooks, and two full-length books of poetry. She says many things motivate her to write: a mood, a memory, the smell of cooking, burning leaves, a windy day, rain, fog, something observed or overheard—and of course, imagination. She lives and writes in Eugene, Oregon. sharonlaskmunson.com

RUSSELL NICHOLS is a speculative fiction writer and endangered journalist. Raised in Richmond, California, he got rid of all his stuff in 2011 to live out of a backpack with his wife, vagabonding around the world ever since. Look for him at russellnichols.com.

ARLENE PLEVIN received her Ph.D. in English from the University of Washington and her MFA in poetry from the University of Iowa. She is an Emeritus Professor of English at Olympic College and worked on sustainability issues and modern slavery. As a former Fulbright Lecturer in Taiwan and a former Fulbright-Nehru Lecturer in India, she has bicycled nearly all over the world and written a now very out of print book on bicycling. Her work has appeared in various publications, including *The Global South, The International Herald Tribune, Columbia: A Magazine for Poetry and Prose, New Mexico Humanities Review, Cabin Fever: Poets at Joaquin Miller's Cabin, Roadshow*, and numerous academic collections. Her poem, "Where I Live," swam around the city of Seattle on light rail, chosen as part of their Poetry on the Buses Program. Plevin has also received a Grant-in-Aid for poetry from the D.C. Commission on the Arts and Humanities and the Commission's Larry Neal Writer's Award for Poetry. She served as an Artist-in-Education in South Dakota and Washington, D.C.

KYLE POTVIN's debut full-length poetry collection is *Loosen* (Hobblebush Books, January 2021). Her chapbook, *Sound Travels on Water*, won the Jean Pedrick Chapbook Award. She is a two-time finalist for the Howard Nemerov Sonnet Award. Her poems have appeared in *Bellevue Literary Review, Tar River Poetry, Rattle, Ecotone*, and *The New York Times*.

CLAUDIA M. REDER is the author of *How to Disappear, a poetic memoir*, (Blue Light Press, 2019). *Uncertain Earth* (Finishing Line Press), and *My Father & Miro* (Bright Hill Press). *How to Disappear* was awarded first prize in the Pinnacle and Feathered Quill awards. She was awarded the Charlotte Newberger Poetry Prize from Lilith Magazine, and two literary fellowships from the Pennsylvania Arts Council. She recently retired from teaching at California State University at Channel Islands. For many years she has been a poet/storyteller in the Schools. Publications include *Alaska Quarterly Review*, *Nimrod*, and *Healing Muse*.

LISA REYNOLDS is a Canadian writer of poetry and short stories. Her works are published internationally in anthologies, literary journals and magazines. She lives in a small community east of Toronto, Ontario.

THOMAS RICHARDSON is the author of the poetry collection *How to Read* (Friendly City Books, 2021). Born in Raleigh, North Carolina, and raised in Columbus, Mississippi, he earned his bachelor's degree from Millsaps College and master's degrees from Vanderbilt University and Mississippi University for Women. He teaches English at The Mississippi School for Mathematics and Science in Columbus, where he resides with his wife Hillary, son Emmett, and their pets.

KAREN RIGBY is the author of *Chinoiserie* (Ahsahta Press.) Her poems have been published in *The London Magazine*, *Australian Book Review*, *Grain*, and other journals. She lives in Arizona. www.karenrigby.com

KIM ROBERTS is the author of six books of poems, most recently *Corona/Crown*, a cross-disciplinary collaboration with photographer Robert Revere (WordTech Editions, 2023). Roberts edited *By Broad Potomac's Shore: Great Poems from the Early Days of our Nation's Capital* (University of Virginia Press, 2020), selected by the East Coast Centers for the Book to represent Washington, DC in the Route 1 Reads program. She is the author of the popular guidebook, *A Literary Guide to Washington, DC: Walking in the Footsteps of American Writers from Francis Scott Key to Zora Neale Hurston* (University of Virginia Press, 2018). Roberts co-curates DC Pride Poem-a-Day each June with filmmaker Jon Gann. http://www.kimroberts.org

WILDERNESS SARCHILD is an award-winning poet and playwright. She is the author of a full-length poetry collection, *Old Women Talking*, published by Passager Books, and the co-author of *Wrinkles, the Musical*, a play about women and aging. She has been featured as Poet of the Week on *Poetry Superhighway*, Poet of the Month at the Brewster Ladies Library, and can be heard reading her poetry on WCAI Poetry Sunday. Her poems have been published in numerous anthologies and literary journals. Wilderness lives in a cottage in the woods in Brewster (Cape Cod), MA, with her husband, poet Chuck Madansky. They are surrounded by wild neighbors that include turkeys, coyote, fox, deer, squirrels, and giant snapping turtles.

ELLEN SAZZMAN is a Pushcart-nominated poet whose work has been recently published in *Atlanta Review, Folio, Delmarva Review, Peregrine, Another Chicago, [PANK], Ekphrastic Review, WSQ, Sow's Ear, Lilith, Common Ground*, and *CALYX*, among others. Her poetry collection, *The Shomer* (2021) was selected as a finalist for the 2020 Blue Lynx Prize, and a semifinalist for the 2020 Elixir Press Antivenom Award, and the 2019 Codhill Press Award. She was awarded first place in the 2022 Dancing Poetry Festival, received an honorable mention in the 2019 Ginsberg poetry contest, was shortlisted for the 2018 O'Donoghue Prize, and was awarded first place in *Poetica's* 2016 Rosenberg poetry competition.

CARLA SCHWARTZ's poems have been widely published, including in her collections *Signs of Marriage, Mother, One More Thing*, and *Intimacy with the Wind*. Learn more at carlapoet.com, or wakewiththesun.blogspot.com or find her on Twitter, Instagram, Threads, Bluesky, or YouTube: @cb99videos. Recent publications include *Banyan Review, The Ear, Channel, Cutthroat, great weather for MEDIA, Inquisitive Eater, New-Verse News, Paterson Literary Review, Remington Review, Sheila-Na-Gig, Silver Birch Online, Triggerfish, The MacGuffin, Verse-Virtual*, and *Leon*. Carla Schwartz is a 2023 recipient of a Massachusetts Cultural Council Grant. Her poem, "Pat Schroeder Was Our Mother," won the 2023 New England Poetry Club E.E. Cummings Prize.

MISTEE ST. CLAIR has been widely published and is a Rasmuson Foundation and Alaska Literary Award grantee. Born and raised in Alaska, she lives with her family in Juneau, where she hikes, writes, wanders the mossy rainforest, and is an editor for the Alaska State Legislature.

MR. TEZOZOMOC is a Los Angeles Chicano Essayist, Poet, and 2009 Oscar Nominated Activist. He has recently published a bilingual book of poems and essays, *I am not your Chihuahua* (Amoxcalco, 2022) and a poetry collection, *Gashes!: Poems and Pain from the halls of injustice* (Floricanto Press, 2019). His work has been featured in *Boundless Anthology, MacroMicroCosm, Healing Hands, Vol 7 Issue #3, Rigorous Journal, Red Earth Productions & Cultural Work, Underwood Press, Mom Egg Review*, and *Los Angeles Poets for Justice*.

ROSS THOMPSON is a writer and Arts Council award recipient from Bangor, Northern Ireland. His debut poetry collection *Threading The Light* is published by Dedalus Press. His work has appeared on television, radio, short films and in a wide range of publications. He wrote and curated *A Silent War*, a collaborative multimedia response to the COVID-19 pandemic. He is currently finishing a second full-length book of poems.

LISA TIMPF is a retired HR and communications professional who lives in Simcoe, Ontario. Her poetry has appeared in *New Myths, Star*Line, Apparition Lit, Third Wednesday, Polar Borealis*, and other venues. You can find out more about Lisa's writing projects at lisatimpf.blogspot.com.

KERRY TRAUTMAN is a lifelong Ohioan whose work has appeared in various anthologies and journals. Her books are *Things That Come in Boxes* (King Craft Press, 2012), *To Have Hoped* (Finishing Line Press, 2015), *Artifacts* (NightBallet Press, 2017), *To be Nonchalantly Alive* (Kelsay Books, 2020) *Marilyn: Self-Portrait, Oil on Canvas* (Gutter Snob Books, 2022), *Unknowable Things* (Roadside Press, 2022), and *Irregulars* (Stanchion Books, 2023).

ANASTASIA VASSOS is a poet living in Boston. She is the author of *Nike Adjusting Her Sandal* (Nixes Mate, 2021). Her chapbook *The Lesser-Known Riddle of the Sphinx* was name a finalist in the Two Sylvias 2021 Chapbook Prize. Her work has appeared in various journals, including *RHINO, SWWIM, Comstock Review,* and *Thrush Poetry Journal*. She is a reader for *Lily Poetry Review*, and a long-distance cyclist.

ELINOR ANN WALKER's work has appeared or is forthcoming in *Cherry Tree, Hayden's Ferry Review, Jet Fuel Review, Nimrod International Journal, Northwest Review, The Penn Review, Pirene's Fountain, Plant-Human Quarterly, Plume, Poet Lore, Shō Poetry Journal, The Shore, The Southern Review, Terrain.org, Verse Daily, West Trade Review*, and elsewhere. She holds a Ph.D. in English from the University of North Carolina-Chapel Hill and prefers to write outside. Her first full-length poetry manuscript, *Meuse is So Close to Muse*, has recently been named a semifinalist for the 2024 Sowell Emerging Writers Prize and the 2023 Charles B. Wheeler Poetry Prize and a finalist for the 2023 Akron Poetry Prize. Find her online at elinorannwalker.com.

LAURA GRACE WELDON has published three poetry collections: *Portals* (Middle Creek 2021), *Blackbird* (Grayson 2019), and *Tending* (Aldrich 2013). She was 2019 Ohio Poet of the Year. Laura works as a book editor, teaches writing, and reads well into the wee hours each night. Connect with her at lauragraceweldon.com

KORY WELLS is the author of *Sugar Fix*, poetry from Terrapin Books. Her writing has been featured on *The Slowdown poetry podcast* and appears in *James Dickey Review, Ruminate, Stirring, The Southern Poetry Anthology*, and elsewhere. A former poet laureate of Murfreesboro, Tennessee, Kory nurtures connection and community through her writing and advocacy for the arts, democracy, afternoon naps, and other good causes. Read more of her work at korywells.com.

MARCELINE WHITE is a Baltimore-based poet and writer whose work has appeared or is forthcoming in *trampset, Culinary Origami, The Heartland Review, Prime Number, The Orchard Review, The Indianapolis Review, Atticus Review, Little Patuxent Review, Gingerbread House, The Free State Review*, and *The Loch Raven Review* and others. Poems have been nominated twice for the Pushcart Prize as well as Best of the Net. She was a recipient of an Aspen Words Fellowship in 2023 and a forthcoming residency with Event Horizon in 2024. When not writing, Marceline can be found serving her two cats, cooking, and telling her son to text her when he arrives at the party. Read more at marcelinewhitewrites.com.

RON WHITEHEAD, author of 24 books and 34 albums, is a poet, writer, editor, publisher, organizer, scholar, and professor. He grew up on a farm in Kentucky. He attended The University of Louisville and University of Oxford. In 2019, Ron was appointed State of Kentucky Beat Poet Laureate by the National Beat Poetry Foundation (serving from 2019-2021), and he was named as the first US citizen and fourth worldwide writer-in-residence, UNESCO Tartu City of Literature international residency program, Estonia.

SCOTT WIGGERMAN is a 2021 inductee into the Texas Institute of Letters. He is the author of three books of poetry, *Leaf and Beak: Sonnets, Presence*, and *Vegetables and Other Relationships*; and the editor of several volumes, including *Wingbeats I & II: Exercises & Practice in Poetry*, and *22 Poems and a Prayer for El Paso*, winner of a NM/AZ Book Award in 2020. With hundreds of poems published in journals around the world, Wiggerman has recently published in *Impossible Archetype, Shot Glass Journal, Modern Haiku, Chrysanthemum*, and *Literature Today*. His website is swig.tripod.com

AMELIA L. WILLIAMS, PhD, medical writer, grew up overseas in a US Foreign Service family with adventurous foodies, and learned to love many cuisines, especially those from the Middle East. She now lives in the foothills of the Blue Ridge Mountains. Her full-length poetry collection, *Species of Concern*, is under contract with Shanti Arts Press, was a finalist for the 2023 Wandering Aengus Press Book Award, and the Word Works Washington Prize. Twice nominated for a Pushcart award, her poems and hybrids have appeared in *TAB, Streetlight Magazine, The Hollins Critic, ANMLY, Rabbit: a journal for nonfiction poetry, Nimrod International Journal, K'in, The Hopper, Poetry South, ArLiJo*, and elsewhere. Learn more at wildink.net.

SUSAN WOLBARST lives in rural Gualala, California, where she works as a reporter for the local (print!) weekly newspaper. Her poetry has been published in *Plainsongs, thewildword.com, pioneertownlit.com, Third Street Review* and others. Five of her poems were published in a recent anthology of nature poems, *Alchemy and Miracles, nature woven into words*. She won second place in the California State Poetry Society's 2022 and 2023 contests. Once upon a time, she wrote a cookbook, *Tasting Gold: A Goldmine of Recipes from Nevada County's Best Restaurants*. When she's not cooking or eating, she enjoys reading, walking on the beach, and messing around in kayaks.

CHRISTOPHER WOODS is a writer and photographer who lives in Chappell Hill, Texas. He has published a novel, *The Dream Patch*, a prose collection, *Under a Riverbed Sky*, and a book of stage monologues for actors, *Heart Speak*. His photographs can be seen in his galleries: christopherwoods.zenfolio.com. His novella, *Hearts in the Dark*, was recently published by Running Wild Press. His poetry chapbook, *What Comes, What Goes*, is from Kelsay Books. He has received residencies from The Ucross Foundation and the Edward Albee Foundation.

ROBERT WYNNE earned his MFA in Creative Writing from Antioch University. A former co-editor of Cider Press Review, he has published six chapbooks, and three full-length books of poetry, the most recent being *Self-Portrait as Odysseus*, published in 2011 by Tebot Bach Press. He's won numerous prizes, and his poetry has appeared in magazines and anthologies throughout North America. He lives in Burleson, TX with his wife and two rambunctious dogs. His online home is rwynne.com.

SARAH YASIN is a self-described corporate dropout working as a cashier in the state of Maine. Her poetry has appeared in various publications including *J Journal, Glass*, and the *Rat's Ass Review*.

Author of one full-length poetry collection and four poetry chapbooks, HIROMI YOSHIDA is a finalist for the New Women's Voices Poetry Prize, and a semifinalist for the Gerald Cable Book Award. While serving as a poetry reader for *Flying Island Journal*, and as secretary of the Writers Guild at Bloomington, she coordinates the Guild's Last Sunday Poetry reading series.

Cover Artist

Hannah McCormick, a native of Starkville, Mississippi, brings the canvas to life with her mastery of color and form. An alumna of the esteemed Savannah College of Art & Design and the University of Mississippi, her education in painting has provided a strong foundation for her evocative works. With years of experience as a commissioned artist, McCormick's pieces have graced numerous galleries, each telling its own visual story. Beyond her personal creations, she imparts her passion for art by providing private lessons, nurturing new talent. Today, she resides in the creative haven of Water Valley, Mississippi, where she has cultivated both a home and a studio, places of retreat and inspiration where she continues to explore the depths of her artistic journey. hannahmccormick.com

Friendly City Books

Production of this book was made possible through the Friendly City Books Community Connection, a special project of the CREATE Foundation.

Friendly City Books is an independent bookstore in Columbus, Mississippi (population 23,000). Founded during the height of the pandemic in 2020, we support our community with literary and cultural programs throughout the year, all under the watchful eye of our bookshop beagle, Scarlet.

Friendly City Books Community Connection is the nonprofit arm of bookstore, established to support literacy and literary arts in Mississippi and throughout the region. Through our efforts, we seek to support essential civic institutions in our area, improve literacy in our public schools, reduce barriers to book access, recognize and develop talented new writers, and enhance the overall quality of life for our neighbors. In our first six months, we handed out over five thousand books in our community. For some, it is the first book they have owned.

With a goal to identify and develop new writers in Mississippi and throughout the South, we relaunched the publishing arm of Friendly City Books as a nonprofit and independent press. This is our third publication after a children's book, *Stretch Like Scarlet* by Emily Liner, and a collection of poetry, *How to Read* by Thomas Richardson.

Learn more about our nonprofit work at friendlycitybooks.com/nonprofit.

Help support literacy and literary arts programs in Mississippi with a contribution to Friendly City Books Community Connection, through the CREATE Foundation:

www.friendlycitybooks.com/support